Sunset
Woodworking Projects I

By the Editors of Sunset Books and Sunset Magazine

Lane Publishing Co. • Menlo Park, California

FOREWORD

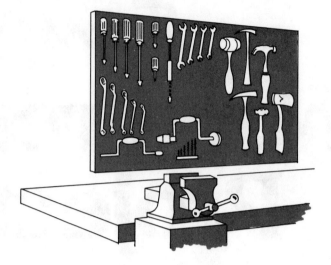

Ideas presented in this book are geared to the needs of beginning or intermediate woodworkers. The 77 projects were chosen for their straightforward designs and techniques. For some projects you'll need only a few simple hand tools and the desire to test your skill. Other projects require power tools and some woodworking knowledge.

All the ideas are accompanied by detailed drawings, helpful photographs, and step-by-step instructions. Projects range from a child's cradle to a portable loom, from a tortilla press to a chest of drawers, from candelabra to coffee or dining tables.

If you're interested in constructing your own indoor or outdoor furniture, children's furniture or toys, hobby and game equipment, household accessories, or garden equipment, these pages will tell you how.

Woodworking Projects I can provide rewarding experiences in working with wood. *Woodworking Projects II,* a companion volume published in 1984, contains many more projects for every skill level.

Sunset Books
    Editor, David E. Clark
    Managing Editor, Elizabeth L. Hogan

Eleventh printing August 1987

CONTENTS

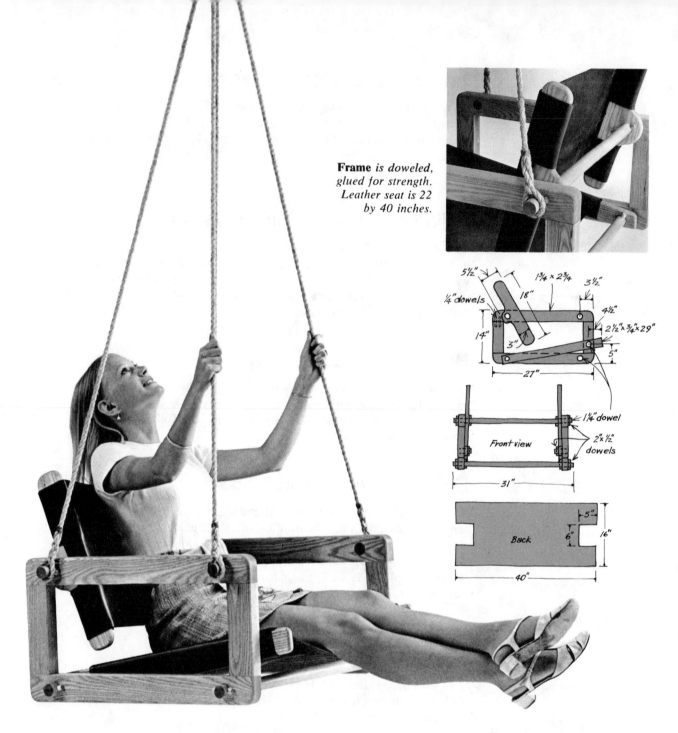

Frame *is doweled, glued for strength. Leather seat is 22 by 40 inches.*

5½"   1¾" × 2¾"   3½"

¼" dowels   18"   4½"

14"   2½" × ¾" × 29"

3"   5"

27"

1¼" dowel

Front view   2" × ½" dowels

31"

5"

Back   6"   16"

40"

Hanging chair for comfort and fun

Bouncing on a stiff overhead spring, this contemporary ash-and-leather chair can offer fun seating either inside your home or under a covered outdoor area.

Ash or a similar hardwood is best. A strong softwood like Douglas fir will work if the dimensions are enlarged for added strength. You could also substitute canvas for the leather seating. Buy the small garage door spring at a junkyard or hardware store.

Although the chair can be built with only hand tools, an electric drill and a saber saw make the difficult work much easier.

The chair's frame is fastened together with ¼-inch dowels and glue. Heavy latigo leather wraps all the way around the ¾-inch-wide side and bottom slats and is tacked to their top edges (see photographs and drawing). Half-inch pegs and cross dowels hold side slats and keep the leather taut.

Give the wood a clear protective finish, splice the four ropes over the protruding dowels as shown, fasten the ropes to the spring, and hang the spring from a strong overhead support.

Design: Norman A. Plate.

Table's Construction *requires straight cuts, but no elaborate joinery. Elegance is due to grooving.*

Glass-topped coffee table

The construction of this coffee table requires no elaborate joinery. It does require precise straight cuts.

The top is a 3-foot square of ¾-inch plate glass with polished edges. However, you can use ½-inch plate or ½-inch crystal. The heavy glass simply lies on the top. The frame, of walnut, is quite simply finished with rubbed-on Danish oil.

First cut the legs and rails to exact length. Then cut the grooves in the legs and lower rails. This can be done rapidly and easily with a ⅜-inch core box bit in a small router that is clamped to the motor of a radial-arm saw.

You can also cut them with a router alone, using some wood blocks for guides. Or you can cut them with a dado blade on a radial arm or table saw (then round the bottoms of the cuts slightly with a rat-tail file). Or you can turn other groovings on a lathe (without square corners).

Drill the dowel holes on a drill press, if possible, however you can use a portable drill by taking care with centering and holding the drill straight. Drill the holes about 1¼ inches deep. Make the dowels fit snug, not tight, and groove them so excess glue can escape.

Design: Virginia Anawalt.

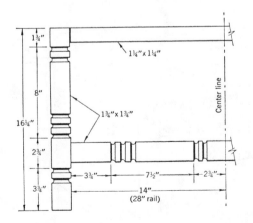

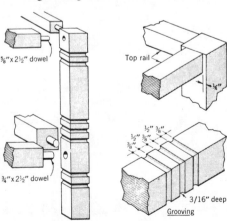

Walnut Frame. *Cut grooves with router or dado blade. Assemble two sides separately, with powder-type resin glue, using clamps or ropes to hold. When dry, glue and clamp other four rails to the legs.*

Table's Height *can be adjusted by using different lengths of tubing recessed in both top and frame.*

Hardwood coffee table suits any décor

Attractive and versatile, this hardwood coffee table blends well with furniture of any period. Although both the top and the frame are made from birch, you could substitute another wood—the top, in fact, can be made from practically any table top material; ½-inch plate glass is a good choice.

To make this table, buy 17 feet of 1″ by 6″ birch for the top and 20 feet of 1¾″ by 1¾″ birch for the frame. You'll also need 15″ of copper or brass tubing, 12 grooved dowels, and a small can of plastic resin glue.

The boards for the top shouldn't show gaps when joined; be sure their edges are straight. Cut them to rough length, leaving a little excess for trimming later. Lay them flat on your working surface. Match the grain but reverse the direction of the growth rings on alternating boards. Apply glue along the long edges; then draw the boards together with bar or pipe clamps (pro-

tect board edges by placing scrap blocks between clamps' jaws and the birch). Sandwich the surface with two or three straightedges clamped across the top and bottom so the top won't bow. After the glue dries, trim the top to finished size and sand the surface smooth.

Next, make the frame. Cut the 1¾″ by 1¾″ pieces to length and assemble them with dowels and glue as illustrated. Insure accurate holes by using a doweling jig, if you have one.

If you alter the table's dimensions or materials, be sure the frame will handle the top's weight; add a middle support if needed. Cut the tubing pieces with a hacksaw or tubing cutter (their length will determine the surface's height). Drill holes for them; then position them in both the top and the frame as illustrated. Sand all wooden parts and add a protective finish.

Design: Christopher S. Payne.

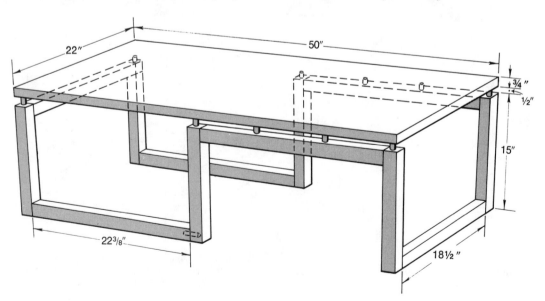

Screw and Glue *fir 1 by 2's to the plywood base. Plug the holes.*

Dowel *the legs to the notched top and cut dowels flush; sand smooth.*

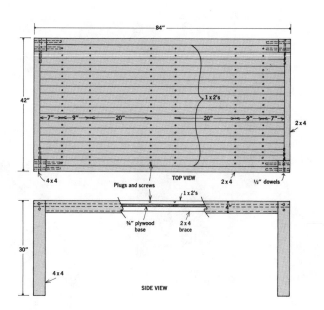

Dining table is big and bold

Seating six or eight, this large Parson's table has a butcher block top. Though a butcher block this large normally would be very expensive, this one is laminated from vertical-grain fir 1 by 2's screwed and glued to a ¾-inch plywood base.

To make the top, have the 1 by 2's milled at the lumberyard to remove rounded edges. Cut the plywood base to size; then coat the 1 by 2's liberally with glue (bottom and sides) and screw them onto the base, squeezing them together with bar or pipe clamps as you work. Countersink the screws ¼ inch and cover them with fir plugs cut from scraps (to make plugs, use a plug-cutter bit in a drill).

If a board warps sideways, straighten it with clamps at points of warpage and drive nails into it from underneath the plywood.

Using a circular saw, trim excess wood around top's perimeter. Screw a 2-by-4 frame to the underside and a second frame of 2 by 4's around the outside of the table. With a handsaw, notch the corners to receive the 4-by-4 legs; chisel away any rough edges.

Cut the legs to length and clamp them into the notches. Mark and drill ½-inch-diameter holes for 9-inch-long dowels as illustrated. If necessary, remove the legs to drill the deep holes.

Clamp the legs in place, squeeze glue into the holes, pound the dowels in, and cut the dowels off flush with the legs. Sand them until smooth.

Use a belt sander for smoothing the table top; then, after fine sanding, finish with oil or varnish.

Design: Peter O. Whiteley.

Chopping block table: a kitchen asset

Chopping block tables are useful and attractive additions to almost any kitchen. This compact table has three main parts: top section, drawer, and leg unit. You can easily adapt the basic design to make a wider or longer chopping block.

The top section is actually a hollow box made from two pieces of 1 by 12 maple and a 24 by 25-inch, ready-made chopping board purchased from a hardware store for under $20.

To cut the board to the right sizes, use a table saw or radial-arm saw fitted with a sharp blade. Saw the chopping board in half lengthwise, with the grain. Use one piece for the top of the box. For the ends, saw the other piece in half, cutting straight across the grain with the blade tilted at a 45° angle.

Cut both ends of the top with the blade tilted at the same 45° angle (see drawing), making it 22¾ inches long. Trim the two ends to 11½-inch lengths (keeping a 45° bevel at the top) and cut the 1 by 12's to lengths of 22¾ inches to match the top.

To make the horizontal cut for the drawer slot, clamp one of the 1 by 12's over the lowered blade of a table saw and raise the blade until it cuts through the wood from below. (When using a radial-arm saw, you would lower the blade into the wood.) Complete that cut by hand and then make the side cuts. Sand all the rough edges. Glue and clamp the table top pieces together, keeping all pieces square. Glue together the drawer pieces, using ¼-inch plywood for the bottom, sides, and back. Clamp until dry.

For the leg unit, rip fir 4 by 4's to 3 by 3 inches and use 2 by 4's for the cross braces. Join the legs in pairs (front and back) with a 2 by 4 cross brace so they will fit inside the length of the top box. Then join these two sections with two parallel 2 by 4's as long as the inside width of the box. The 2 by 4's, centered 6¼ inches apart, serve both as cross braces and as drawer guides. Glue and nail all joints in the leg section. Set the nails and fill the holes.

Small Table *appears solid but actually is hollow. Storage drawer is hidden below.*

Apply glue to the top and sides of the legs and slip the table top over the legs. Wipe off all excess glue. Drill ¼-inch holes and insert dowels as shown in the drawing. Use glue and short lengths of ¼-inch doweling to join the drawer to the precut front piece.

Decorative ¾-inch dowels can be added to the sides as shown. After it's thoroughly sanded, the table top should be coated with mineral oil.

Design: Peter O. Whiteley.

Drawer, *cut into the table's front, stores recipes, knives.*

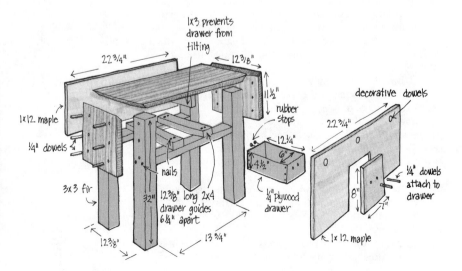

Table Top *rests directly on legs that are notched together at the center.*

Patio Table *holds hibachi in recessed center, can be taken apart for storage.*

Patio table dismantles for winter storage

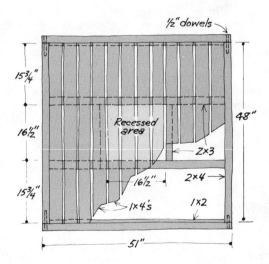

The recessed area in the center of this patio table can hold a small barbecue or a planter. The whole table is easily taken apart and stored out of the way and out of the weather. This one was built of vertical grain Douglas fir, but you could substitute redwood or cedar, both of which can stand more exposure.

For the table-top frame, join the 2 by 4's with a pair of ½-inch dowels in each corner as shown in the drawing. Nail the 2 by 3 cross braces between the 2 by 4's, spaced as shown and depressed ¾ inch below the top.

Two shorter 2 by 3's nailed between the cross braces outline the recessed center square. End supports for the top pieces are 1 by 2's nailed ¾ inch below the top surfaces of the longer 2 by 4's.

For the top, the 1 by 4's are spaced about ½ inch apart. Each of the four 1 by 4's that cross the center is actually three short lengths; the middle piece of each is recessed. Fasten the recessed boards in place, nailing horizontally through the cross braces with 5-penny finishing nails. Nail all the top boards to the 2 by 3 cross braces and horizontally through the outer frame.

The 2 by 4 leg sections run diagonally from corner to corner. The two bottom pieces are notched in the center—one on the top, the other on the bottom. The 18-inch-high legs are fastened to the bottom pieces with ½-inch dowels.

Countersink nails and plug holes with wood putty, sanding before finishing with oil or with plastic sealer.

Design: Peter O. Whiteley.

Eight Minutes *is all the time required to build this garden bench. Simplicity is part of its charm.*

Garden bench made with two boards

Besides the straightforward design of this garden bench, other advantages are its imperviousness to weather and its stability; it's heavy enough that it won't tilt even on soft ground. All members are of rough-cut, 2-inch redwood, which is a full 2 inches or more in thickness. Rough-cut cedar would serve equally well.

You can make the bench with just three saw cuts: Cut a 50-inch length of 2 by 4 for the leg brace; cut two 13-inch lengths from an 8-foot plank, and you then have both legs and top. A handsaw will do the job; but most lumberyards will make these cuts for you if you wish.

Best width for the plank top is 14 to 16 inches. But you may find that some of the more commonly available 12-inch stock in your local yard is over 13 inches wide (rough-cut lumber varies in width) and is wide enough for this use.

The legs of this bench were secured to the 2 by 4 brace with two galvanized 20-penny common nails at each end and were toenailed to the top from below with 16-penny nails. For more positive joinery, brush waterproof glue on the joints before assembling, or use ¼ by 5-inch galvanized lag screws and washers in drilled holes.

Design: George F. Malone.

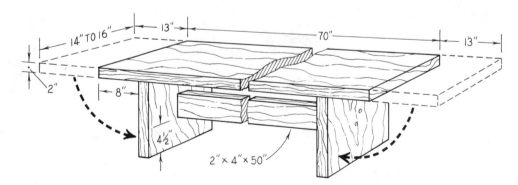

Choose Rough-Cut Boards *that are uniform in width and thickness, and preferably, fairly dry. The completed garden bench requires no finish or stain, can be left outside to weather naturally.*

Camp Table *is also food locker. Cabinet latches hold the drop leaves in place to protect food when you are away from camp. Leg and leaf supports can be removed so that folded table will fit in car trunk.*

Camp table that folds for storage

This folding table, with folding stools or chairs, will accommodate four persons comfortably in camp. It is equally handy as a "kitchen counter" alongside a picnic table, leaving that table clear for eating.

When the leaves are down, the large locker protects your food. The leaves are held up by two wood supports (see drawing at right) that slide through openings in the table ends. The legs and leaf supports, when removed, can be carried separately, or you can notch the locker's middle partition as shown to carry them inside. The drop leaves can be held down with cabinet latches, or you can simply secure both with a 5-foot web strap around the locker.

Assemble with screws or glue and nails and place four furniture glides on the underside. Obtain two fairly large "garage-door" handles for the ends.

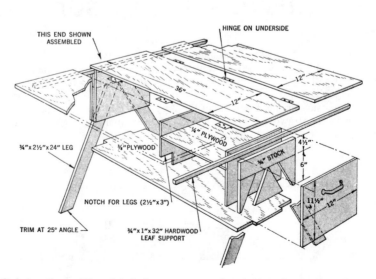

THIS END SHOWN ASSEMBLED

HINGE ON UNDERSIDE

36"

12"

12"

¼" PLYWOOD

⅜" PLYWOOD

¾"x2½"x24" LEG

¾" STOCK

4½"

6"

NOTCH FOR LEGS (2½"x3")

11½"

12"

TRIM AT 25° ANGLE

¾"x1"x32" HARDWOOD LEAF SUPPORT

Construction. *All unlabeled parts are made of ½-inch exterior plywood. Large handles at two ends will also serve as handy towel bars.*

For Pool or Patio, *these comfortable lounges are easy to make from pine 1 by 4's nailed to 2 by 8 Douglas fir runners. Casters underneath let them roll easily to capture the sun.*

Platforms to sun on. . .surprisingly comfortable

Beside a pool or on a deck, these sunning platforms are comfortable, sturdy, and portable. Construction is simple. They consist of eighteen 30-inch 1 by 4's nailed to two 6-foot-long 2 by 8's.

Use a handsaw or saber saw to cut the 2 by 8 runners as shown in the drawing below. Space the slats ½ inch from each other (a ½-inch plywood block makes a good

spacer) and use 16d finishing nails (countersunk and puttied) to attach the slats.

Small ball-type casters on the bottom of the runners make it possible to move the lounges toward the sun or out of sight. The units can be stained, oiled, painted, or left natural after a thorough sanding. Any soft wood can be used; pine is a good choice.

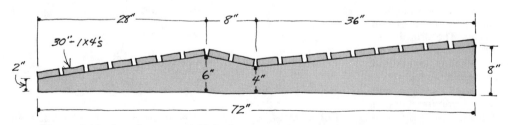

Plywood *block makes a good ½-inch spacer when attaching pine slats to runners.*

Mahogany Headboard *fits any bed; it's fastened to frame with ½-inch angle irons inside the posts.*

Bed headboard with a traditional look

Traditional flavor characterizes this queen-size headboard, made entirely of finished ⅞-inch-thick Philippine mahogany. You can easily modify the design by using other hardwoods, such as oak, birch, or walnut, or by altering the dimensions to fit a different bed frame or mattress.

This headboard's back is actually three boards glued together: one 13 inches wide and two 11 inches wide. Be sure to choose quality boards—edges should be straight so they will fit closely together without showing gaps. End posts are made from three 3½-inch-wide boards of ⅞-inch mahogany glued together flat to form posts 2⅝ inches thick.

Before gluing, cut the boards to rough length. Leave a little extra for final trimming.

Lay the back boards edge to edge on a flat surface, matching the grain as closely as possible. Spread glue along their edges and clamp them tightly together with bar or pipe clamps.

While the glue dries, screw the two 4-inch-wide strips (you could use ½-inch plywood) to the back. Then cut the curve across the top of the headboard as illustrated.

Glue together the end posts and, when dry, secure them to the back with ⅜-inch dowels and glue. Use a doweling

jig to insure straight holes when drilling. The top trim blocks are cut from leftover mahogany.

The headboard shown, after a good sanding, was given three coats of clear polyurethane varnish.

Design: Howard Crittenden.

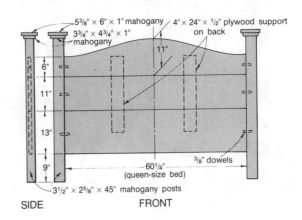

5⅜″ × 6″ × 1″ mahogany   4″ × 24″ × ½″ plywood support on back
3¾″ × 4¾″ × 1″ mahogany
11″
6″
11″
13″
9″
60¼″ (queen-size bed)
⅜″ dowels
3½″ × 2⅝″ × 45″ mahogany posts
SIDE   FRONT

Magazines go on a stair rail

This shallow wooden rack was designed to hold a collection of magazines, pamphlets, and art portfolios, and to dress up what used to be a somewhat bare part of the room. The rack was attached to an existing wrought iron railing next to a stairwell. You could adapt this idea to suit your own stair railing or simply attach it to a wall.

The compartments are only 1⅞ inches deep, so even floppy magazines can be displayed vertically. Top sections, right and left, are 12 inches high. Sections below them are 14½ inches high, for larger magazines. The center panel contains an 8½-inch-high section for small pamphlets and books, and an 18-inch-high section for art and other tall publications.

In the installation shown here, the trick was to start with ½-inch plywood panels, one for each of three divisions of the railing. These rest on the bottom rail and are held from behind by screws fitted through holes drilled in the metal rail uprights.

All the lumber, except for the ply, is 1 by 3's (actually ¾ by 2½ inch), some of it ripped down to 1⅞-inch width to make the four inner verticals and the shelves (keep the leftover thin strips for cross members).

Nail a full-width vertical side piece to each outermost edge of the rack. Attach a pair of the narrower vertical pieces beside each inner railing post, with screws through the rear of the plywood. Then nail shelves to these verticals and reinforce each with two screws from behind.

Nail 1 by 3's to the top of the rack and in front of each shelf. Finally, add the thin cross members to keep magazines upright.

End View *shows how rack fills space between top and bottom members of stair rail. Magazines are kept upright.*

Shallow Wood Rack *for magazines, pamphlets, and art books is placed against wrought-iron stair rail; provides band of warmth and color next to an otherwise bare section of wall.*

Lightweight but strong bookcase was finished with dark stain, then clear varnish. Disassembled (photo at right), the bookcase takes up very little space for storing, and it is easy to move about.

This bookcase comes apart

Since you can mass-produce each of the three different parts of this bookshelf, you can build the whole thing in a few hours.

THE L-SHAPED SHELVES

For each of the three shelves, you need two 6-foot lengths of 1 by 12-inch shelving. First, square off and trim all pieces to the same length. Then saw one end of each piece at a 45° angle, taking care that this angle is accurate so the assembled shelves will match. You can leave the other ends square or trim them as was done here (see photo above right).

Lay out the shelf pieces and choose the surfaces you want to face up (since pieces match, you can switch them around). Join each pair of pieces together with four or five corrugated fasteners, driven into the bottom side.

THE DOWEL SUPPORTS

The dowel holes in all three shelves must align so the supports will stand straight. On the first shelf, measure in 12 inches from each end, and then measure 12 inches toward each end from the inside corner. At these points, draw lines, across the shelf width (using a T-square) and mark two centers for drilling on each line 2 inches in from each edge. When all eight corners are marked, drill holes 1⅜ inches in diameter. Use this shelf as a guide for holes in the other two shelves.

Using 1⅜-inch diameter closet dowel, cut supports 1½ inches longer than the planned height of the top shelf level (example is 35 inches high). Drill ¼-inch holes 2½ inches from the top and 2¾ inches from the bottom of each dowel section to hold metal pins that will support shelves (extra space at the bottom makes bookcase easier to clean under). For the middle shelf, drill one set of holes, or several sets at various levels so you can adjust shelf height.

THE STEEL PINS

Use a hacksaw to cut 24 steel pins, 3 inches long, from ¼-inch diameter, zinc-finished stock. Smooth off cut ends with an emery wheel or file. Insert the dowels to support the shelves.

Spacious Desk *is made by using two module boxes, adding wood bases below and a 10½-foot plywood top. Two boxes on wall above double storage. Desk top is 2 feet deep; knee space is 2 feet square.*

Desk and storage using module boxes

Cut from 4 by 8-foot plywood panels with little waste, these large module boxes can be stacked up from the floor and topped for a counter, desk, or work table. The boxes can also be hung on a wall with only four wood screws, to provide additional storage space. Adding the optional middle partition shown in the sketches provides non-sagging shelves. You simply cut the long shelves in half, use one piece for the partition and the others again for shelves. With butt joints throughout, the simple construction facilitates the building of several boxes at one time.

A power saw is the one shop tool required; it's needed to insure square edges. If you do not have a power saw available, many lumberyards will make these straight cuts for you, sawing the pieces to size for a small charge when you buy the plywood.

All wood parts come from ¾-inch fir plywood, excepting the back of ⅜-inch (preferable) or ¼-inch plywood. Two 4 by 8-foot panels of ¾-inch plywood laid out as shown in the cutting plan will give two complete boxes with little waste. One box will have one long interior shelf; the other, two.

Before assembling the boxes, drill three pairs of ¼-inch holes for adjustable shelf brackets (for three shelf positions) in each end and any middle partitions. Space the holes 2 inches in from front and back of the boxes, and 4 inches apart (vertically). Drill the holes only ½ inch deep in the ends, but drill through the middle partitions—for brackets on both sides.

For the storage units above the desk, hang each box on a wall with four No. 12 wood screws through the ⅜-inch plywood back, through any plaster or similar surface, and into two wall studs at about 32 inches apart. Locate two of the screws about 2 inches below the top of the box, the other two about 6 inches up from the bottom. Place washers under their heads and use screws long enough to go an inch or more into the studs.

Place 1 by 2-inch spacers between a desk or workbench top and the box (see desk detail at right). This gives clearance for the cabinet doors and also allows using a wider, more attractive edge trim on the top.

Paint just the doors (the easiest part) to give these cabinets a well-finished appearance. An excellent finish to prevent against mars and scratches is a paste stain wax. Many door handles are fairly expensive; the ones shown in the photo are not. They are lacquered ¾ by 2 by 7-inch pieces of pine, with sides cut at a 30° bevel on a table saw.

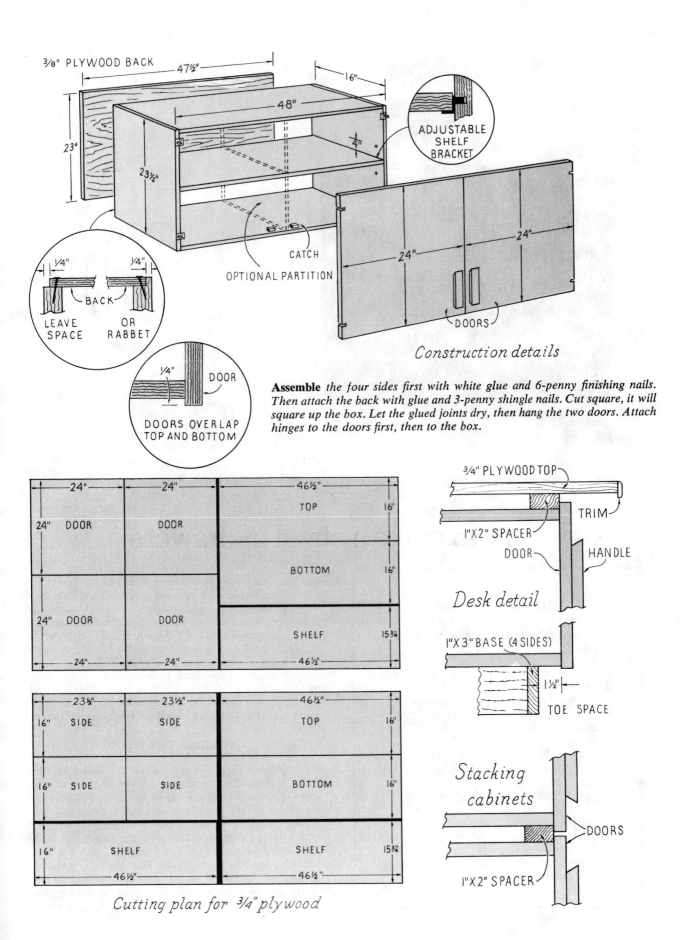

3/8" PLYWOOD BACK

47½"

16"

48"

23"

23½"

4"

ADJUSTABLE SHELF BRACKET

¼" ¼"

BACK

LEAVE SPACE

OR RABBET

¼"

DOOR

DOORS OVERLAP TOP AND BOTTOM

24"

24"

DOORS

CATCH

OPTIONAL PARTITION

Construction details

Assemble *the four sides first with white glue and 6-penny finishing nails. Then attach the back with glue and 3-penny shingle nails. Cut square, it will square up the box. Let the glued joints dry, then hang the two doors. Attach hinges to the doors first, then to the box.*

24"	24"	46½"
24" DOOR	DOOR	TOP 16"
24" DOOR	DOOR	BOTTOM 16"
24"	24"	SHELF 15¾"
		46½"

23½"	23½"	46½"
16" SIDE	SIDE	TOP 16"
16" SIDE	SIDE	BOTTOM 16"
16" SHELF	SHELF	SHELF 15¾"
46½"		46½"

Cutting plan for ¾" plywood

¾" PLYWOOD TOP

TRIM

1"X2" SPACER

DOOR

HANDLE

Desk detail

1"X3" BASE (4 SIDES)

1½"

TOE SPACE

Stacking cabinets

DOORS

1"X2" SPACER

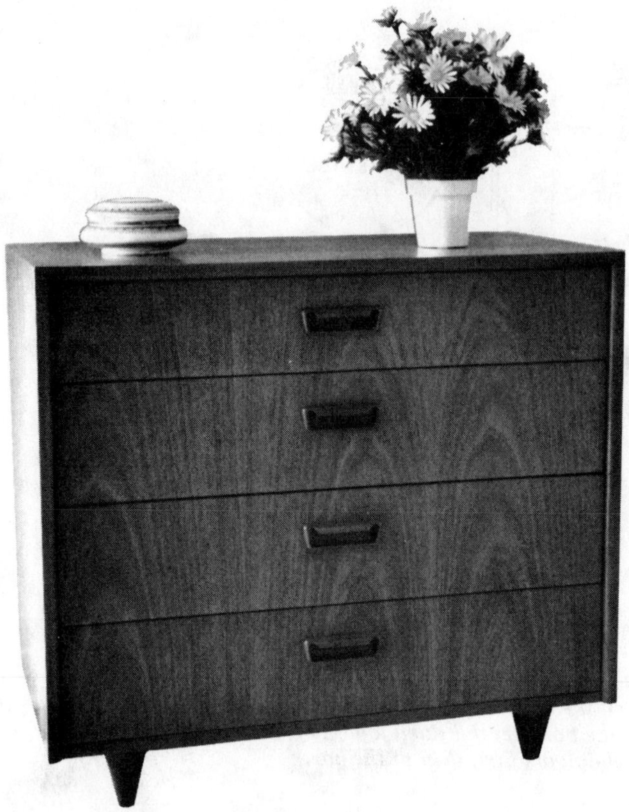

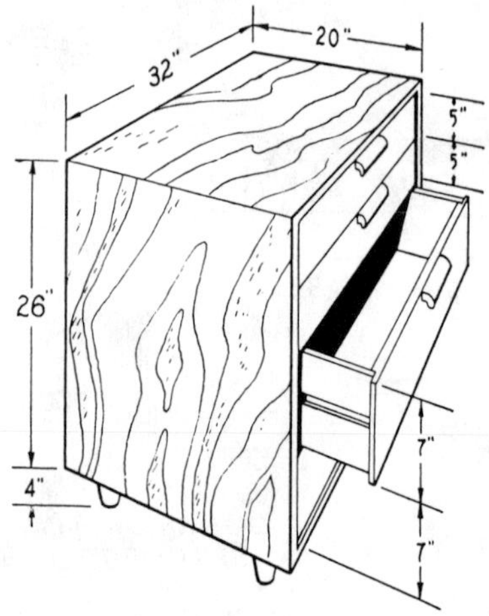

Step-by-Step Construction *details below for this chest of drawers make it a good project for the new power tool owner. Dimensions at right are fraction of inch oversize to allow for fitting at assembly time.*

How to make a chest of drawers

BILL OF MATERIALS

Item	Size
¾-inch plywood or laminated boards	
1 top	32⅛" x 20"
2 sides	25⅝" x 20"
2 drawer fronts	5" x 30¼"
2 drawer fronts	7" x 30¼"
½-inch plywood or lumber	
4 drawer sides	5" x 18¾"
4 drawer sides	7" x 18¾"
2 drawer backs	28¾" x 4⅜"
2 drawer backs	28¾" x 6⅜"
¼-inch plywood or hardboard	
1 back of frame	31½" x 25½"
4 drawer bottoms	28⅞" x 18⅞"
scrap lumber	
2 bottom rails	¾" x 4" x 31¼"
8 glide rails	¾" x ¾" x 18½"
2 bumper strips	¼" x ¼" x 23"
stock for legs and drawer pulls	2" x 2" x 16"

For the new power tool owner, this chest of drawers is a good project, since it requires a great many cuts, rabbeted grooves, and special joints. The same principles of construction can be applied to any drawer assembly, freestanding or built-in. To the left is a list of materials required. Look carefully for any usable pieces you might have in your scrap pile, then make a careful list of exactly what you will have to buy. With everything on hand before you start, you will be able to utilize each setting of your saw blade or dado assembly for the maximum number of similar cutting or rabbeting operations.

BUILDING THE FRAME

First, decide which type of joint to use in fitting together top and sides. The drawing at the top of the next page shows four of the most common joints. This project uses the rabbeted joint since it is easy to cut. Once you have all the pieces cut to size, follow these steps:

Set the dado blade assembly to the depth (⅜ inch) and width of cut (13/16 inch) required for the joint between the top and sides. The 1/16-inch fractional surplus will allow for finish sanding to provide a perfectly smooth surface where sides join the the top. Run both ends of the top piece through the dado assembly.

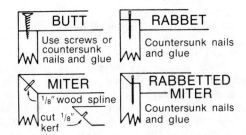

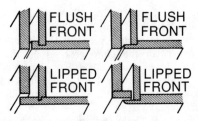

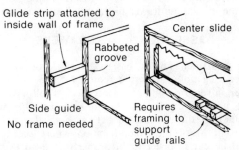

Four Choices *for drawer assembly.*

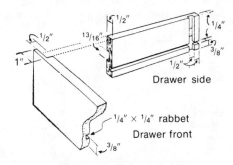

Side Guide *is sufficient except for wide drawers. Center slide prevents binding if drawer is pulled off center.*

Leave the dado setting untouched, and run the bottom edges of the two side pieces through to rabbet for the front and back bottom rails.

In order to fit in the back panel flush, you need to rabbet the back edges of both side pieces and the top. Leave dado blade setting the same and move fence so that blades will cut rabbeted recess ⅜ inch deep, ¼ inch wide.

No more rabbeting cuts are required for the frame members. Before you assemble them, check all pieces to see that they fit properly.

Apply glue to the rabbeted ends of the top piece. Prop one side up against a sturdy vertical surface—or have someone hold it—then carefully fit the top in place. Lift the other side and gently lay the top on. Partially drive 4 finishing nails down through the top into each side piece. Drive the nails slowly, continually checking to see that they aren't out of line. (As long as the head is exposed, the nail can easily be removed.)

Since the frame will wobble at this stage, you have to work quickly to get the bottom rails and back panel in place before your glue begins to set.

Apply glue to the ends of the two bottom rails. Tip the frame on one side and fit the bottom rails in place. Be sure to locate rail at least ¼ inch in from back edge to allow for back panel. Drive and set several nails to anchor each rail in place while the glue dries. (Whenever you have to put a side or a top on the floor while you are working, set it on a blanket or pad so that small stones or particles won't dent or mar the finished surface.) Turn the frame and cinch the rails on the other side.

Next, apply glue to the two edges of the rabbet in the back of the top and side panels, and set the ¼-inch back panel in place. You need only 3 or 4 small brads per side to hold this in place until the glue sets up. The combination of the bottom rails and back panel will stabilize and should square up the frame. Double-check the squareness with a 2-foot square, then set the frame aside while you assemble the drawers.

CUTTING AND ASSEMBLING THE DRAWERS

Some methods of constructing drawers and slides call for the skill of a professional cabinet maker, but those shown in the two sketches at the top of the next column are within the realm of the average home craftsman.

Regardless of which method you choose, remember that each individual drawer will normally require the same number of rabbet grooves and cuts. Check back to the list of materials required to build the 4 drawers. When you have all these cut to size, determine exactly where rabbet cuts and grooves are required on each separate piece.

The sketch below shows the cuts required on the side pieces and front of a typical drawer. Mark these on 1 set of drawer pieces. Then, as you set up your blade assembly for each separate cut, repeat the action on the other 3 pieces. (The bottoms and backs need no special rabbet grooves.)

The procedure used to make this project is as follows: Set up your dado blades to cut the ¼-inch rabbet for the drawer bottom on both fronts and sides, but not on the backs. The guide fence should be set ⅜ inches from the blade to allow for necessary bearing below the drawer bottom. (Depth of cut should be ¼ inch, as shown in the sketch above.)

Before you go on to cut each piece, test the width of this groove by forcing a scrap piece of the ¼-inch drawer bottom material into the groove. The bottom should fit snugly but allow some movement when forced. Rabbet the bottom edges of all sides and fronts with this one setting of the saw blade.

Change dado blade assembly for the ½-inch rabbet to let the back into the sides. Set the rip fence ½ inch from blade assembly (depth of cut should be ¼ inch), and make the 8 required cuts. (Remember that only 4 of these drawer sides will be identical. The other 4 will be reversed. You can verify this statement and avoid mistakes by actually sketching all of the required cuts on 2 opposite drawer sides.)

Change the dado assembly to cut the ¾-inch rabbet (¼ inch deep) for the glide grooves on the outside surface of the drawer sides. Add 2 or 3 paper washers between the dado blades so that the width of the opening will allow enough play for the ¾-inch glide strip to operate smoothly.

Change depth of blade setting to ½ inch and make the 1-inch rabbet on the side of each drawer front. These four different settings are the only ones required to prepare the individual drawer pieces for final assembly.

ASSEMBLING THE DRAWERS

Most craftsmen find it easiest to work on only one drawer at a time. Stack the required 5 pieces for each drawer in separate piles, then proceed as follows:

Set up one drawer front and side. Fit the drawer bottom into the ¼-inch rabbet on both the side and the front. Mark the exact location where the bottom should be cut in order to fit properly at both the back and opposite side. Cut the drawer bottom to size; then fit it loosely in place.

Since the drawer back must exactly equal the width of the drawer bottom, it can be cut to fit at the same time you cut the bottom. Assemble the rest of the drawer without glue as a final check on fit.

Place the drawer front face down on a padded surface. Fit the drawer bottom in place, applying glue to the ¼-inch rabbet at several points. (This will keep the drawer front from warping and bowing out at the front.) Apply glue to drawer front or side, as shown in sketch below, and fit side in place. Drive 3 nails to fasten side

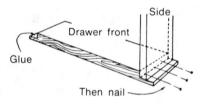

to front. Follow the same procedure for the opposite drawer side, gluing and nailing it to the drawer front.

Next, apply glue to back ends and bottom of the back piece and fit it in place. Several nails driven from the outside of the drawer side will lock the back in place. Turn drawer upside down and drive several nails through the bottom into the drawer back.

LOCATING DRAWER GLIDES

First, prepare the glide strips by drilling 3 holes in each strip. They should be countersunk so that the screws won't protrude past the surface. If you use 1-inch, flat head screws, countersink should be approximately ⅜ inch. See sketch at top of next column.

The location for each glide could be calculated and the glide installed before you assemble the frame, but you might run the risk of an error in calculation. Instead, most craftsmen prefer to install the glides after the

drawers have been assembled. This way you can check the exact location for each pair of glides by the following procedure:

Start with the bottom drawer and fit 2 of the ¾-inch glides loosely in place in the rabbeted grooves on the outside surface of each drawer side. Set the drawer carefully in place in the frame so that the glides don't fall out. Shim up the drawer front ³⁄₃₂ inch so that it doesn't rest on the bottom brace, and sight down through the crack at the side of the drawer front. Mark on each side of the frame the exact location for each glide; then remove the drawer and use the 2-foot square to mark glide lines inside the frame. See details in sketch below.

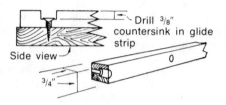

Screw the two bottom glides in place, and fit the drawer back in place. If the drawer binds, sand or plane down the glide rail until it slides smoothly and easily.

Follow the same procedure with the other 3 drawers, fitting the drawer loosely in place and marking the location each time before you screw on the glides. If your drawer fronts are cut exactly to the measurements listed, there will be approximately a ³⁄₃₂-inch space between drawers and above and below the top and bottom drawer. Don't forget to account for this as you fit each successive drawer in place.

Two bumper strips, nailed and glued to the glide rails as shown in the sketch below, will allow the drawers to

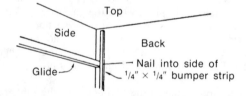

recess about ⅜ inch back from the front edge of the frame. By changing the dimensions of these strips, you could make the drawers flush or recess them even further.

LEGS AND DRAWER PULLS

The round, tapered wood legs used on this chest of drawers were turned out on a lathe. You could build a simple skirt-type frame of 1-by-3-inch lumber, substitute square tapered legs, or choose from a variety of ready-made metal legs.

Hardware stores and builders' supply stores carry a wide range of both metal and wood pulls and handles.

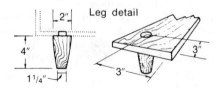

Leg detail

Easily Reached *by children, clothes rack is simply made with six pieces held together by screws and dowel.*

A portable clothes rack for children

One way to encourage children to hang up their clothes is to provide a clothes rod that can easily be reached. The easy-to-make clothes rack shown here is 36 inches high, a good height for pre-schoolers. It is also portable and can be used for various other purposes, such as a gaily decorated Christmas stocking rack (see photo on the left below).

The rack is simply constructed, consisting of six pieces held together by four screws and a dowel piece. After completion, apply a wax or clear finish.

Decorated *with ribbon and fir boughs, clothes rack also serves as place to hang stockings at Christmas.*

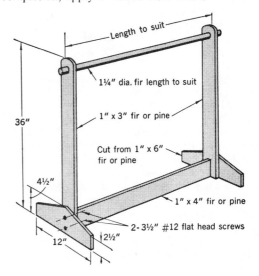

Length to suit

1¼" dia. fir length to suit

1" x 3" fir or pine

Cut from 1" x 6" fir or pine

36"

1" x 4" fir or pine

4½"

2 - 3½" #12 flat head screws

12"

2½"

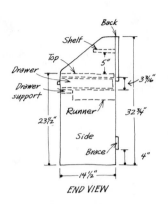

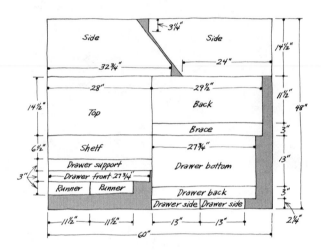

End View *of child's desk is cut-away, showing all the assembly plans and construction measurements.*

Plywood Layout *shows how to cut out the pieces. Remember to allow for the saw kerf.*

Simple *to build and scaled for a child under 12, this desk has shelf on top, wide drawer underneath.*

Child's desk—build it in an afternoon

A child will find it easy to call this simple, scaled-down desk his very own. It's inexpensive to build and sturdy enough to withstand rough handling, and you can build it in an afternoon using only hand tools.

All pieces can be cut from a 4 by 5-foot sheet of ¾-inch plywood. Before buying a full 4 by 8-foot sheet, ask your lumber dealer if he has any cut plywood in stock. Choose plywood graded A-B.

When marking the pieces for cutting, don't attempt to measure them all at once; the width of your saw cut (kerf) throws off the measurements.

First, lay out the sides and make the long cut to the outside of your line. Then saw through the center edge shared by the other pieces. Measure and mark each remaining piece before cutting it out.

Assemble the pieces with 1½-inch finishing nails and white glue. Nail the back and the brace to the sides; then nail in the top and shelf.

Next, assemble the drawer and then nail the drawer runners to the sides (use 1¼-inch finishing nails here). Attach the horizontal drawer support with 1½-inch nails. Add a drawer pull of scrap wood.

If you like, cover the front edges of the shelf, desk top, and drawer support with ¾-inch wood-trim veneer tape or molding (this was not done on the desk pictured).

Set nails, fill any blemishes, sand (rounding front edges of sides), and paint.

Design: J. W. Hoyt.

Versatile indoor-outdoor stools

Simple, versatile, and inexpensive, these indoor-outdoor stools can be made from a single sheet of plywood. They make good furniture for children, are lightweight, and could hardly be easier to build. Just a 2-foot square of ½-inch plywood yields a complete stool.

Each stool is 17 inches square and stands approximately 10½ inches high. If you wish to use a cushion, you can add a ½ by 1-inch hardwood trim around the top's edges, which will give a ½-inch-high rim to keep the cushion in place.

To start, draw the cutting pattern carefully on heavy paper and transfer it to each 2-foot plywood square with carbon paper or pin pricks. If making several stools, you can have the lumberyard cut your plywood to uniform 2-foot squares. Cut the legs and top from each square with a power or hand saw.

Each leg abuts on and is nailed to the inner end of the next leg. Assemble with glue and just two 3-penny shingle nails in each leg. Before the glue dries, turn the assembled legs right side up on a smooth surface and attach the top. As you glue and nail on the top (use 6-penny finishing nails), the legs will level themselves evenly. Finish the stools as you prefer with paint, varnish, or stain wax.

Stable and Sturdy *stools are handy to seat a group outside or inside. They also make good step stools for kitchen or utility area.*

Underside. *Glue and nail the legs together, then glue and nail them to the top. Finish with paint, varnish.*

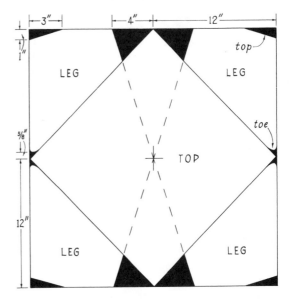

Pattern *for cutting from 2-foot squares of plywood. Only shaded areas are wasted. Assemble with glue, nails.*

Two-Year Crib *has a front gate that drops for easy access. Mattress in photo is at top level (there are two other choices). Crib is lightweight and narrow enough to roll through standard-sized doorways.*

A crib and a five-level child's bed

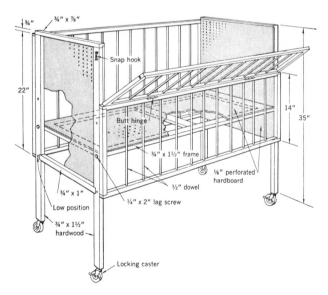

Framing Members *not identified are of 1 by 1-inch (actual size) stock. Mattress here is at middle level.*

Both beds on these two pages are handsome and fairly easy to build. The detailed diagrams and instructions will help you in completing the project.

TWO-YEAR CRIB

Get a crib mattress before you begin to construct this crib. The smaller crib mattress sizes vary considerably and the size of your mattress will govern some of the dimensions. The crib shown above has a 20 by 41-inch mattress; the mattress platform is exactly the same size.

Glue the perforated hardboard of the platform to its frame. Also glue the two end pieces of perforated hardboard to their frames, which are the same width as the platform. Rabbet the top pieces of the end frames to receive and protect the upper ends of the hardboard panels. A 2 by 8-foot piece of hardboard furnishes all three panels.

You can use any sound softwood or hardwood lumber for the frame, but the ½-inch dowels should be hardwood. With a sharp wood bit, drill ⅝-inch-deep holes in the side frames for the dowels and assemble the frame corners with glue and screws. Just use screws, but ample

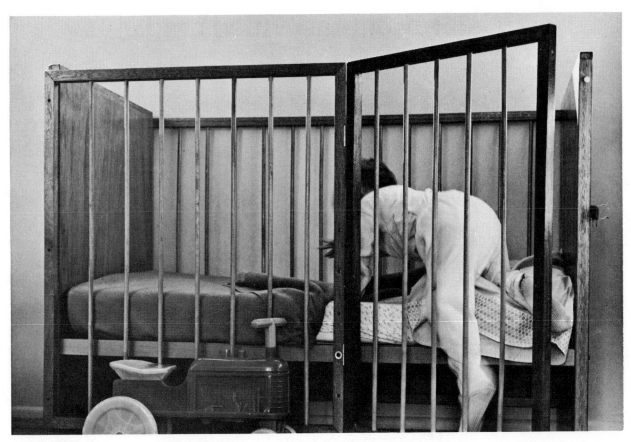

Child's Bed *is much larger than crib. Here its mattress is at the next-to-lowest of five different levels. With the mattress placed low, the bed becomes a youth-bed, but child cannot roll off onto floor.*

ones, to secure the side frames to the end frames. This will allow you to disassemble the crib and pack it flat for shipping or storage.

Use locking-type casters on the front legs so the baby's movements will not move the crib. Hold the drop gate up with hooks and eyes of the type that have spring catches, so the baby will not be able to loosen them.

You can easily attach decorations to the perforated ends. A small wood block mounted with two or three screws through the perforations provides a base to which you can attach a mobile. Finish the crib in any way you like, as long as the finish is non-toxic. The crib shown here has clear acrylic spray paint on the hardboard and wax on the framing.

CHILD'S BED

One 28-inch-wide, mahogany (lauan), hollow-core, flush interior door cut in half gives you both ends of this crib. Cap the two cut ends with glued-on ¾ by 1⅜ by 28-inch pieces of mahogany; these ends go at the top of the crib.

The mattress platform, 28 by 52¾ inches, fits one of the standard-size large crib mattresses. Note that you place its framing members on edge. Assemble with glue and nails.

Five carriage bolts, two at each end and one on the gate side, hold the platform in any of five positions.

Assemble the two doweled sides in the same manner

as those of the smaller crib but use heavier ⅝-inch doweling. Attach a secure child-proof latch to the gate and tack two small rubber bumpers to the end of the crib behind the gate to prevent slamming. As with the crib, complete the bed with any non-toxic finish.

Design: Richard E. Londgren.

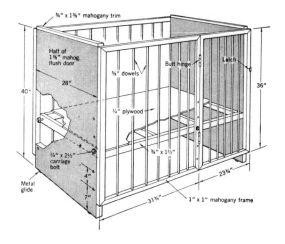

Construction of Bed. *Carriage bolts at each end hold the platform securely in any of five positions.*

A sturdy old-fashioned cradle

Sturdy, yet light enough to be moved about, this charming cradle is high enough for adults to attend to youngsters without stooping. It is assembled almost entirely with screws, so that it can be disassembled for storing away compactly.

The cradle hangs on two metal stair-rail brackets (available at builders' hardware stores). Size of the brackets you're able to buy will determine the length of the cradle bed. The two small straps that loop around the brackets are secured to the top edges of the cradle with 3-inch-long wood screws.

Wood parts are cut from ¾-inch Philippine mahogany plywood. Cover all exposed plywood edges with mahogany veneer tape, purchased at a lumberyard and cemented on.

You can draw the curves with a compass or with a pencil and a length of string. The curved parts can be cut out with a jigsaw, band saw, scroll saw, or router. The single cross piece is notched at its ends for its small reinforcing blocks, which are glued permanently to it; then all are screwed to the wood ends.

Design: Gordon Brofft.

Gentle Rocking Motion *of this cradle delights tiny occupant. Assembled with screws, the cradle is easily disassembled for compact storage.*

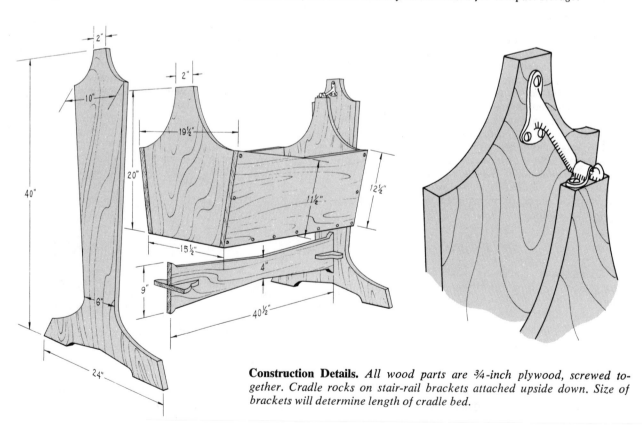

Construction Details. *All wood parts are ¾-inch plywood, screwed together. Cradle rocks on stair-rail brackets attached upside down. Size of brackets will determine length of cradle bed.*

Her cradle is curved plywood

Both lightweight and functional, this attractive cradle is constructed in an unusual way. A single piece of pre-grooved, 5/16-inch plywood is slotted to receive the ends, each made of 3/8-inch plywood. The ends hold the bent plywood in shape and are also its rockers.

To make a similar cradle, first lay a sheet of 3/8-inch plywood on a floor and mark it for the cuts shown in the end-view diagram (shown below). Use a long wood strip (with a nail in one end and pencil at the other) as a compass to scribe the 57½-inch-radius curves. Cut out this piece (it is a C-member of an end) with a saber saw, jigsaw, or band saw and use it as a pattern to cut five more identical pieces.

Next, cut four of these pieces in two along the 11-inch-radius curve shown in the end-view diagram. This cutting will give you four A-members and four B-members. Trim the four A-members ¼ inch along the same 11-inch-radius curve (to leave room for the plywood bed). Now, glue two B-members in place on each side of the two C-members. White glue is easy to apply and of ample strength for this project.

For the cradle bed, use a 41 by 41-inch piece of 5/16-inch plywood. Score it as indicated in the photograph by making parallel cuts with a power saw, 1/8-inch deep on 1-inch spacings (make cuts parallel to grain of plywood surface). Test-bend this plywood bed to shape and use one of the two partially assembled ends to measure how long you should make the two 3/8-inch slots by which the ends and the bed are fitted together.

After cutting the slots, slip the two partially assembled ends through them and use glue and small nails (predrill nails in 5/16-inch plywood to avoid splitting) to secure the bent bed to the B-members of the ends. Then use glue to secure the four A-members in place inside the cradle on the C-members. These A-members should cover the small nails.

When the glue is dry, cut the hand holes in the two ends. Fill any voids in the plywood with wood filler and finish the plywood edges with wood tape, if desired. Attach a ¼ by 1¼-inch hardwood strip to the bottom edge of each end.

Architect: Daniel H. Goltz.

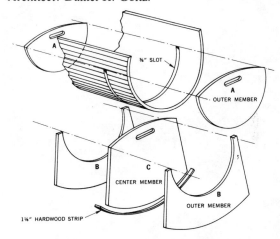

End Assembly. *Member C slides through slot in 5/16-inch plywood. A and B members are glued, nailed to sides of C.*

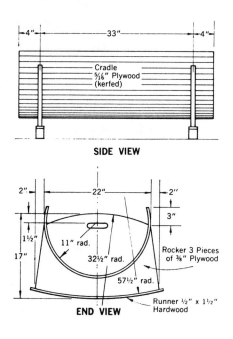

Construction *dimensions. All parts except hardwood runners are plywood.*

Generous-Sized, *this cradle is yet lightweight for carrying. Cradle's center of gravity is very low, and it is virtually tip-proof.*

Giant Block *is a toy box on wheels—just the right size for preschool children. One of two, it rolls into cubicle at bottom of playhouse. These children find lots to do, up, down, in or out of magical cupboard.*

It's a cupboard, toy wall, puppet theater

Your children and their friends can spend hours clambering on, over, and through this curious piece of furniture. You can let them give it a name. It's a cupboard, a marionette theater, a submarine, a toy box, and several other things that they'll discover or decide upon as they climb around on it.

This project was built to provide storage space for dolls, books, and toys. The owner's children liked hiding in the closet, so he built a cupboard with folding bench, where they could not only hide, but look out through the periscope to check on their mother. They also liked to climb on chairs, beds, and dressers, so he included a ladder and a roped-in deck topside. The rolling toy boxes replace one they used to drag around the room, turning up rugs and leaving tracks on the floor. The marionette

theater is popular since the children can act out bedtime stories such as Red Riding Hood when they feel like it, or just play with the curtains when they don't.

Construction is simple and straightforward. Sides, top, bottom, door, and shelves are of ¾-inch plywood. The back is ¼-inch plywood. Ladder is vertical grain fir.

For the railing on top you can use 2-inch dowels and a 1 by 2 fir strip, or fancier turned uprights in place of dowels. You'll also need a length of rope for the railing, 4 strap hinges for the toy boxes, 4 cabinet hinges and 2 magnetic catches for bench and door, and 8 casters that measure 2 to 3 inches top to bottom. A short length of traverse rod holds the curtains. The lazy Susans are the 16-inch size available in many hardware stores and intended for kitchen cabinets.

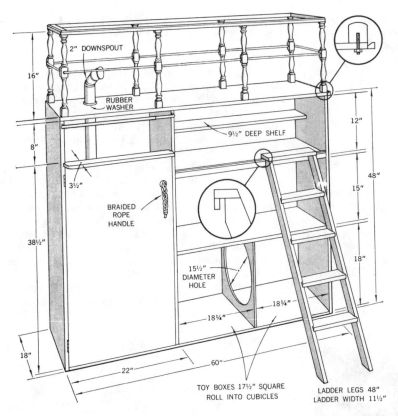

2" DOWNSPOUT

16"

RUBBER
WASHER

8"

9½" DEEP SHELF

3½"

BRAIDED
ROPE
HANDLE

38½"

15½"
DIAMETER
HOLE

18"

18¼"

18¼"

22"

60"

TOY BOXES 17½" SQUARE
ROLL INTO CUBICLES

12"

48"

15"

18"

LADDER LEGS 48"
LADDER WIDTH 11½"

Change Dimensions *to suit your child. Toy boxes have beveled cubicle edges so boxes roll in. Bench in cupboard folds up, locks on magnetic catch.*

Ladder *hooks onto side when not in use; boxes roll out with easy pull.*

Lazy Susan *doll house has rooms behind front door.*

Puppet Master *is revealed during exciting performance.*

Periscope *has mirrors top and bottom, eye hole in side.*

This furniture can grow with the child

Sturdy and fun to use, this play table and its chairs have another advantage, too: Their height can be increased as a child grows.

The set is made of birch and birch plywood; but you could use practically any hardwood or softwood, including redwood or pine.

You'll need a power saw for the mortise and tenon joints of the sides (you could simplify this joinery, if you wished, by using miter or half-lap joints). If you intend to leave the furniture outdoors, you might eliminate the seat upholstery and use plastic cushions that can be taken indoors at night.

Make the sides of the chairs and of the table base exactly the same, 13 inches square. Assemble the four pieces of each side with glue (no nails or screws); use water-proof glue if the furniture is to go outdoors.

To form a chair, assemble three of the sides with four ⅜-inch dowels and glue, as shown—two dowels at each corner. This furniture is blind-doweled, so that the doweling does not extend through the outer piece. It's easier, however, to drill completely through that piece, and just smooth down the exposed end of the doweling.

After upholstering the chair seats and painting the wood sides, install the seats: Attach each one with four small steel corner reinforcing plates and wood screws or sheet metal screws.

(Later on, when you need to raise the seats, you simply relocate these angle plates higher up the sides.) The table base's four sides are assembled the same way, with glue and two dowels at each corner. In the top of the base and in the underside of the table top, drill four holes for the dowels supporting the top. Glue these dowels only lightly, so they can be knocked loose later and be replaced with longer dowels to raise the table's height.

This birch furniture was finished with a water-clear wood sealer, and then with a water-clear lacquer.

Design: Gordon Hammond.

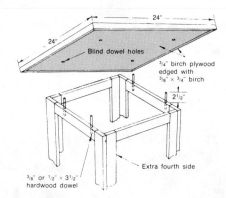

Table Legs are chair sides with a fourth added. To raise top, replace supporting dowels with longer ones.

Tables and Chairs *are useful both indoors and on the lawn. As child grows, chair seats, table top are raised.*

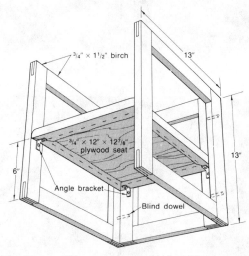

Chair's Three Sides *are assembled with two ⅜-inch dowels placed at each corner. Glue all joinery.*

Five-Foot Alligator (*1 foot longer than his friend*) *is made from 16 sections that slither as he rolls.*

Wiggling animals follow children

Children enjoy pulling toys around. And the wooden animals pictured here wiggle and lazily curl as they go. They're easy and inexpensive to construct with basic home woodworking tools. You build in the wiggle by making two identical body shapes, cutting the two into vertical sections, and then sandwiching canvas between them. Following the same steps, you can build animals of almost any shape and size.

You'll need two pieces of 1 by 12-inch lumber for the body and two 12-inch-long 2 by 3's for the legs (crosspieces which hold the wheels). Keeping the shape simple, draw the outline of an animal body on one of the 1 by 12's. Draw vertical lines to divide the animal into sections where the body might logically bend. (Sections, to which you'll attach crosspieces, should be at least 3 inches wide.)

Next, place an equal length of 1 by 12 under the outlined body and temporarily fasten the two boards together by driving two small nails (just deep enough to hold) through each marked section. Saw apart the vertical sections and then cut along the body outline with a coping saw or band saw. (Cut notches for the crosspieces.) Take the nails out of each section.

With a saw or power sander, remove at least a 45° wedge from adjacent section edges (see drawing).

Cut out a silhouette of lightweight canvas about ¼ inch smaller all around than the animal's outline. On a table, lay out the pieces for one animal body with the insides facing up. Leave a 1/32-inch space between wooden sections.

Center the canvas on top of the pieces, then carefully position the other set of wooden sections on top of the canvas. Drive several 4-penny finishing nails into each section, checking for alignment as you work.

For the legs, drill holes in the 2 by 3's to accept a caster housing at each end; attach the legs to the body with 3-inch wood screws through their centers. Countersink nails, fill holes with wood putty, and then sand and paint. Add ears and a tail if you wish. Screw a small eyehook into the animal's nose for a pull cord; add wheels or casters to the crosspieces.

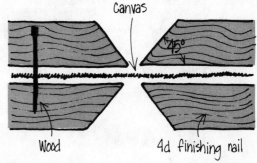

Nail Canvas *tightly between all the wooden sections. Angled edges let animals make sharp turns.*

Docile Elephant *follows owner everywhere.*

Friendly Elephant *sports floppy leather ears and swinging wooden trunk.*

Children can ride these rocking animals

A rocking animal has a special quality that captures a child's imagination. These simple rocking beasts, made from wood and other natural materials, are as fascinating to a child as a sophisticated mechanical toy.

The construction method for all these animals is a simple gluing and doweling process that requires little skill and only a few hand tools—but if you have them, a ¼-inch electric drill and a band saw or saber saw can save you time. These animals were made from vertical grain Douglas fir.

The bodies of all animals shown are basically the same—made by joining 1½-inch-thick end pieces to 1 by 2's with ⅜-inch dowels. The size of the end pieces depends upon the size of the animal. The giraffe's body is slightly different from that of the other animals because two circles form the end pieces and 18-inch-long 2 by 2's form the legs.

Starting at the middle of the animal's back, join 1 by 2's to end pieces with 2-inch lengths of ⅜-inch dowels; drill ⅜-inch holes, apply plastic resin glue liberally, and pound in the dowels. Keep end pieces parallel to each other and perpendicular to the 1 by 2's while working around the animal's back.

The lion's head is cut from a 4 by 6 (see drawing). For eyes, fasten wooden pulls with dowels. Two floor mop heads attached with nails create the mane.

The giraffe's head, also cut from a 4 by 6 block, perches atop a 3-foot-long neck, made from a 2 by 4. The neck is doweled to the body. The ears, cut from a single piece of leather, are glued into a slot between neck and head. Two dowels join each 18-inch-long 2 by 2 leg to a rocker and two more dowels join each leg to a body end piece.

The elephant's head looks more complicated than the others but consists simply of a series of 4 by 6 blocks, cut as shown in the drawing. You make the trunk from seven 2-inch-thick blocks cut from a 4 by 4 and tapered down with a saw and wood rasp until rounded at the small end. Drill two holes through each block so it can be strung onto ropes; tie knots between the blocks to separate them.

Though Douglas fir is a relatively durable softwood, it splinters. If you use it, round all corners and do a thorough sanding job. The animals can be painted, stained, oiled, or left unfinished.

Design: Rick Morrall.

Make Bodies by doweling 1 by 2's to 2 by 12's. Length of 1 by 2's varies for each animal: elephant—22 inches; lion—18 inches; giraffe—16 inches.

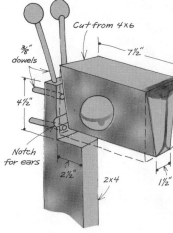

Cut from 4x6

3/8" dowels

7½"

4½"

Notch for ears

2½"

1"

2x4

1½"

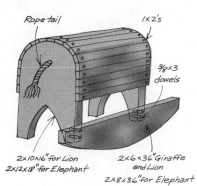

Rope tail

1x2's

3/8x3 dowels

2x10x16" for Lion
2x12x18" for Elephant

2x6x36" Giraffe and Lion
2x8x36" for Elephant

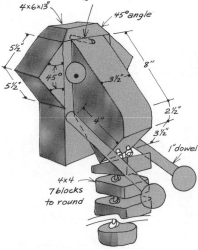

4x6x13"

3/8" dowel

45° angle

5½"

5½"

45°

3½"

8"

4"

2½"

3½"

1" dowel

4x4
7 blocks to round

2x4

All dowels 3/8"

8"

9"

45° angle

10"

2x4

Cut from 4x6

Popeyed Lion *has mane made from two mops nailed to its head. Rockers can be rounded or flattened to regulate motion.*

Long-Necked Giraffe, *with wood-stain spots, has 7½-inch diameter body.*

Stallion Gallops *along when he is pulled by the long string. (See color photograph on front cover.)*

"Cam critters" bob as they roll

Compared to today's highly sophisticated playthings, wooden pull toys that bob up and down appear naively simple. Yet they continue to amuse young children.

The ones shown here can be cut out with a jigsaw from 1-inch softwood and ¼-inch dowels. The dowels serve as axles and cross braces at each end of the frame.

The bobbing motion is created by an elliptical cam, fixed off center on the front axle. The animal's front portion rests on the cam and moves up and down as the wheels turn. The rear axle passes through ⅜-inch holes in the frame and in the rear part of the animal; the animal pivots on the rear axle.

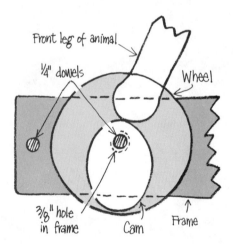

Front Section *cut-away shows forward leg in down position. Attach cam to axle; it moves with the wheel.*

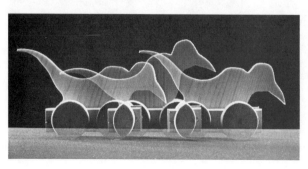

Bird Bobs *up and down when pulled. Triple exposure shows bird's motion.*

Cozy Turtle *has a weighted head and tail that bob and nod when he rocks and rolls.*

Soft-shell turtle offers a rolling ride

This cushioned turtle is as great for a reptile rodeo as it is for quiet indoor play. The shredded foam (four pounds of it) stuffed under the vinyl-cloth shell makes an excellent pad for reclining or pouncing on. Two pairs of rockers allow the beast to rock forward and back, as well as from side to side.

The base for the shell is a ½-inch-thick plywood oval roughly 32 by 36 inches. To make the pad, pile the foam on the plywood; then place over it a piece of vinyl-cloth about 40 by 48 inches. Use tacks every inch or so to attach the cloth to the plywood's underside; gather the cloth as you go, cutting off the extra.

Cut out the rockers, making sure that the bottoms are flat in the middle. Make two notches in each rocker, cutting from the bottom up on two rockers and from the top down on the other two so the two sets can intersect each other, forming four cross-lap joints. Glue and screw the rockers to the plywood base.

Cut head and tail shapes out of wood scraps. Attach a piece of all-thread rod and several nuts to the head for balance. Use eyebolts and eye screws to mount the head and tail on the body.

For a smoother ride, you can tack rope to the underside of the rockers with small brads. On the side-to-side rockers, start the rope a few inches away from rocker intersections so it won't touch the floor when the turtle is rocking from front to back.

Add a rope for reins, paint exposed wood yellow, paint on a turtle's face—and some youngster should be able to rock around the clock.

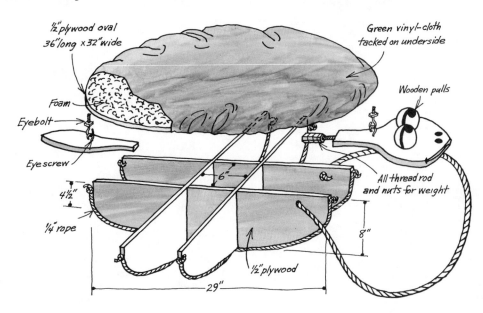

Hobby Horse *bucks (if weight is put far forward), can also be "walked" along.*

Bronco Power *comes from a garage door spring. Tighten turnbuckle (see diagram) for stiffer action. Galloping motion stays horizontally level.*

Wheels and springs for hobbyhorse power

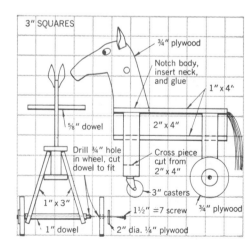

3" SQUARES

¾" plywood

Notch body, insert neck, and glue

1" x 4"

⅝" dowel

2" x 4"

Drill ¾" hole in wheel, cut dowel to fit

Cross piece cut from 2" x 4"

3" casters

1" x 3"

1½" =7 screw

¾" plywood

1" dowel

2" dia. ¼" plywood

Hobby Horse Parts, *for animal at left above, are easily assembled. Wheels are casters and plywood disks.*

Few toys come with such a sound guarantee of fun as hobbyhorses. This fact goes far to account for their ancient lineage and the great diversity of their design. The two horses shown on these two pages are easy to make and will delight both the toddler and the older youngster.

A HORSE ON WHEELS

A sturdy sawhorse is the frame for this pony. Front wheels are large casters for maneuverability, rear wheels are ¾-inch plywood disks that rotate on a 1-inch dowel axle fixed in holes drilled at an angle through the legs. Small ¼-inch plywood disks glued and screwed to the dowel ends hold the wheels on. The ears are leather triangles, glued and nailed to the ¾-inch plywood head. The tail is rope, glued and nailed into a ½-inch slot in the upright 2 by 4. All members are attached with white glue and nails. See the diagram at left for details.

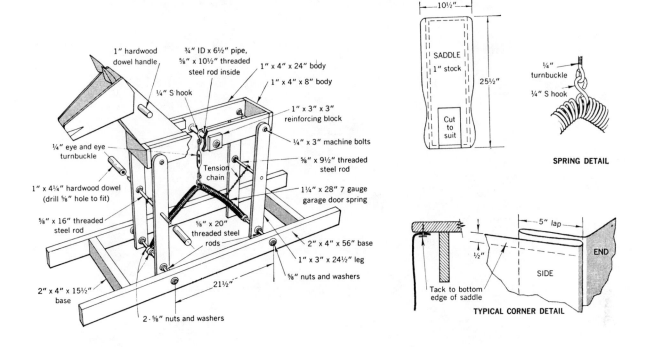

Bronco Materials: *About 8½ feet of 1 by 3-inch finished hardwood for the legs, 5½ feet of 1 by 4 finished clear fir for the body, and about 12 feet of 2 by 4 for the base. Assemble with white glue and nails.*

A HORSE ON A SPRING

All hardware for this horse is available at a well stocked hardware store. Cut the legs and round the tops. Drill a ¼-inch hole in each leg equidistant from sides and top, a ⅝-inch hole 22 inches below it (about 1½ inches from the bottom), and a ⅝-inch hole halfway between.

Cut the body pieces and drill ¼-inch holes in the side pieces where the legs will join them. Glue on the reinforcing blocks and drill a ⅝-inch hole through each. Assemble the body with white glue and nails; run the rod through the pipe, and secure it with nuts and washers.

Bolt legs to the body, using 1½-inch-diameter washers between legs and body.

Assemble the base with white glue and nails, and drill ⅝-inch holes in the side pieces to receive the lower rods.

Assemble the spring mechanism by bending the spring in half sharply, to force the coils apart in the middle. Holding the spring in a bent position, have a helper slip an S hook under two coils (see detail). Crimp hook closed around coils.

Run lower rods through base, legs, and spring, threading on nuts and washers as you go. Leave nuts loose for the time being. Attach rods midway up the legs with nuts and washers on the inside only, and glue the drilled dowels over the protruding ends of the front rod.

Attach an S hook to the pipe, then insert both hooks in the turnbuckle eyes and crimp closed. Tighten the turnbuckle to hold the horse upright. Attach the two chains (they keep the spring from binding when the horse rocks) by bolting around the bar at one end and running a small wire under a coil of the spring and through a link of the chain at the other. Tighten all nuts except those flanking the 2 by 4's and the spring. Leave these slightly loose so the rods can move with the legs. Lock all nuts in place by dabbing a little white glue on the threads.

Use scrap lumber to build the head and neck to whatever design you wish. This one is attached to the body with wood blocks, glue, and nails. Cut the saddle board to fit around the neck. This board extends out far enough from the sides to permit the skirt, which hangs from it, to clear the hardware below. Four screws, countersunk, secure the saddle to the frame.

The horse's skirt serves to cover the moving parts at top and to fill out the body to horselike proportions. Make it from a 15-inch by 10-inch strip of 8-ounce duck, or other heavy, closely woven fabric. Baste in the pleats along the top (see sketch) and tack the skirt along the underside of the saddle with upholstery tacks, starting at the back and following the saddle's edge as you work forward to the neck opening. At that point, screw down the saddle and tack the rest of the material to the front of the body. You'll have enough material left for an overlap in front.

The tail is a length of untwisted rope.

If the weight of your youngster rocks the horse too far, so that it swings down to the base and stays there, limit the arc by drilling a ¼-inch hole in front and back body pieces, attaching two ¼-inch eyebolts, eyes inside, and running a loop of stout clothesline from each eyebolt to the rod midway up the leg on the opposite side. Adjust the length of the line to stop the horse before it reaches the collapsing point.

Easel Frame *is 60 inches high, 32½ inches wide. Backboards are 25½ by 37½ inches. Height of backboards is fully adjustable at 2½-inch intervals.*

Two can work at this easel

Two children can paint at this double easel without getting in each other's way. They put both sides to use.

Each painter has his own set of paints—dry tempera, mixed with water and kept in square, lidded, plastic refrigerator cartons that hang unspillably in a 4½-inch wide shelf—and a good supply of 24 by 36-inch paper, punched at top and hung on three dowels. (A 2 by 3-foot blackboard also fits over the dowels.) Brushes can be left temporarily in paint jars, supported upright by the notched brush rack.

The easel's frame is of hardwood; the two sides are hinged along the top so that the easel can fold flat when wing nuts holding the crosspieces are loosened. The backboards are ⅝-inch plywood, trimmed with smoothed redwood for soft, finished edges.

Each board attaches to the frame by two dowels protruding from its back and resting in holes in the leg members. Four such holes running at 2½-inch intervals along each leg make the height of the boards adjustable (in the photograph they are shown in their lowest position, 25 inches from the floor).

Design: W. W. Mayfield.

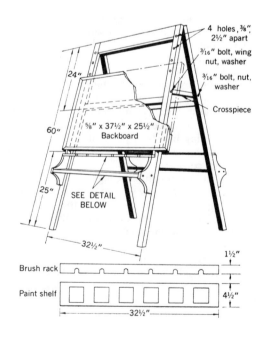

38

Drafting table folds against the wall

Designed to fold up on a garage wall so it will clear car doors and stay clean, this drafting table is big enough for large-scale drawing jobs. With these features and an attractive design, it could serve equally well inside the house. The top is a ready-made drafting board. You can substitute ¾-inch plywood (the lumber-core type gives the smoothest edges) and reduce the size of the board and cabinet if desired.

Make the shallow cabinet of 1 by 4's softwood or hardwood. Before assembling it with glue and nails, notch the two inner uprights for their three slats and drill a ½-inch hole through each for the removable dowel. This dowel is simply slipped sideways to remove; it helps hold large sheets of paper upright.

Attach the board to the cabinet with a piano hinge, set about ¼ inch back from the edge of the drafting board. Then the edge of the board will serve as a fence along the top of the cabinet in both the up and down positions, giving a handy pencil shelf.

The cabinet has no back but is simply attached to the plywood garage wall with four small metal corner brackets. On a plaster wall, you may find it easier to include a ¼-inch plywood or hardboard back and drive screws or nails through that back into the studs.

Install the folding legs last. If you change the size of the drafting table, keep the two halves of each leg equal in length (between hinging points) and attach them to the board and cabinet at equal distances from the piano hinge. Then they will fold up smoothly and lock down rigidly in their open position.

Folded Down, *the table is out of the way, and neither the top nor the stored paper and other materials gather dust.*

Table Swings Up *from the wall. It's big and steady and has no legs in the way. Paper stores upright, underneath in shallow cabinet.*

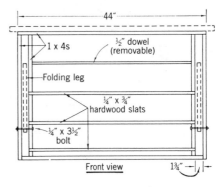

Front view

- 44"
- 1 x 4s
- ½" dowel (removable)
- Folding leg
- ¼" x ¾" hardwood slats
- ¼" x 3½" bolt
- 1¾"

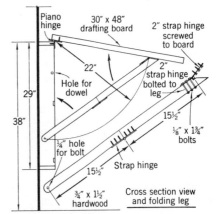

Cross section view and folding leg

- Piano hinge
- 30" x 48" drafting board
- 2" strap hinge screwed to board
- 22"
- 2" strap hinge bolted to leg
- Hole for dowel
- 29"
- 38"
- 15½"
- ⅛" x 1¾" bolts
- ¼" hole for bolt
- 15½"
- Strap hinge
- ¾" x 1½" hardwood

Attach *braces' upper hinges to the drafting board; then bolt to the legs.*

Rolled Outside *to the edge of a lawn where shavings and sawdust can be raked into bare soil beyond, this full-height, roomy workbench is handy and useful for home craftsmen of any age.*

A workbench that rolls outdoors

You can build this portable workbench complete with drawers, as shown here, or you can simplify the construction considerably by substituting another cabinet door. The drawers, however, are very useful.

Before assembling the base cabinet and legs, slot the ¾-inch plywood of the left side and middle partition for the drawers, if they are to be included, and cut holes for the drawer locks. Make drawers whatever height you wish, to fit your tools.

For the secret compartment (for prized tools), simply cut the bottom drawer about 6 inches shorter in length, and make an open-topped box to fit in behind it, as shown.

The drawer lock is a hardwood bar with small hardwood blocks glued and screwed to it. When raised, they clear the drawer slots; when all drawers are fully closed, they drop into notches in the drawer bottoms. To lock the bottom drawer, a metal corner angle, bolted to the bar, drops into a notch in the top of that drawer's side. Cut a deep notch in the cabinet shelf for the locking bar, so it can be installed at any time, and screw a wood stop to the underside of the shelf there to hold the bar snugly.

The wide overhang of the bench top on the left side will accept most wood vises along its front edge without complications, and also serves as the handle when moving the bench. Cut out the edge trim there for the vise, so its inner jaws will be flush with the top's edge. Paint the cabinet as you wish. Give the bench top one thin coat of clear sealer to prevent staining and finish with wax.

Large Wheels *roll easily over rough surfaces and lawn. Bench locks up completely, includes a secret drawer.*

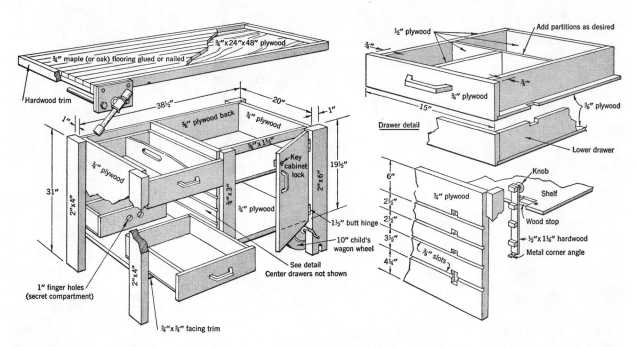

The diagram labels:

- ¾"×24"×48" plywood
- ¾" maple (or oak) flooring glued or nailed
- Hardwood trim
- 38½"
- ⅜" plywood back
- 20"
- ¾" plywood
- 1"
- 1"
- ¾" plywood
- ¾"×1½"
- Key cabinet lock
- 19½"
- 2"×6"
- 31"
- 2"×4"
- ¾"×3"
- ¾" plywood
- 2"×4"
- 1" finger holes (secret compartment)
- ¾"×¾" facing trim
- 1½" butt hinge
- 10" child's wagon wheel
- See detail
- Center drawers not shown
- ½" plywood
- ¾"
- Add partitions as desired
- ¾" plywood
- ⅜"
- 15"
- ⅜" plywood
- Drawer detail
- Lower drawer
- 6"
- ¾" plywood
- Knob
- Shelf
- 2½"
- 2½"
- Wood stop
- 3½"
- ½"×1¼" hardwood
- 4¼"
- ⅜" slots
- Metal corner angle

Assemble *base cabinet first with glue, nails, and screws; next, the plywood top, then hardwood top. The four upper drawers are ⅜-inch "breadboards" with plywood fronts, sliding in the slots.*

Metal Vise, *bolted to a plywood square and short piece of 2 by 4, stores in a large cabinet to the right.*

Most-Used Tools *are kept in the upper drawer. Removed, it becomes handy tool box you can take anywhere.*

Wood Bar *inside cabinet drops and locks drawers when closed. Key lock on the cabinet door secures all.*

Wheel Assembly *(two 10-inch wheels on ½-inch axle) slips into bottom notches to use, stores on upper notches.*

Portable Workbench *can be taken right to the job. It can be used for pounding, sawing, and sitting or as a stepstool or toolbox. The tray below carries tools needed at the moment.*

Use it as a seat, workbench, tool carrier

Carpenters build handy little benches like this one to use in various ways around a job, particularly when doing indoor finishing. Such a bench can be equally useful for your maintenance jobs around the house.

You can use it as a seat and as a compact workbench —for sawing, pounding, drilling, and the like. And it's a stable stepstool, just high enough to let you reach an 8-foot ceiling. Its tray makes a convenient carrier for the tools you may be using at the moment.

Dimensions of this example are given in the drawing at right, but you need not follow them exactly. Every carpenter's bench you see will be somewhat different from the others, because each utilized the scrap lumber on hand. A piece of 1 by 12 is the best size for the top. Keep the legs out close to the ends, so the bench won't tip when you stand on one end. Choose the lightest boards you have on hand, so the completed bench will be easily portable. Use glue as well as nails on the simple joints.

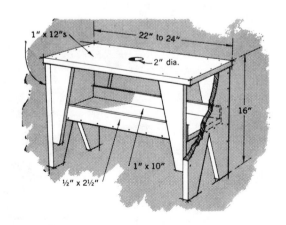

Construction Details. *Alter the dimensions to fit the scrap lumber you have on hand. Note carrying hole in top.*

You can fold away this workbench

This solid little bench can be used for all work except heavy pounding. If you're planning a workbench for an area where space is at a premium, this fold-away design may be your answer.

The bench shown here is designed especially for woodworking and repairs, but also could be used as a garden workbench, an outdoor buffet table, a place for barbecue equipment, a place to unload a car.

THE PLATFORM

The platform is built of 2 by 6-inch tongue-and-groove fir planks, with the joints glued. Nail two 1 by 4-inch boards across the underside, 6 inches in from each end and flush at the front and back; these are stiffeners, and foundations for the pipe legs and the platform's hinges. For a good working surface, nail and glue a piece of ⅛-inch tempered hardboard to the platform top, cut to the latter's dimensions.

THE ELECTRICAL OUTLET

For the maximum of convenience in using power tools (no cords underfoot or across the work surface), this example has a combination 110 and 220-volt electrical side-bracket surface outlet box. The side bracket on the box is screwed to a small block of ¾-inch-thick plywood nailed to the platform underside. The two plugs are mounted flush with the front edge of the platform.

The bench folds down against an open wall and the outlet box and its flexible steel conduit are positioned to fit between the studs. A single metal strap holds the conduit in place against the platform's underside.

THE LEGS AND HINGES

Center the pipe leg flanges on the 1 by 4's, 6 inches back from the front edge. Cut two equal pieces of galvanized 1-inch-diameter steel pipe to lengths that will give the bench the height you want when the legs are screwed in place. (Be sure to compensate for the added height that the platform, flanges, and leg caps will give.) With the bench attached to the wall, you'll find that you can lift it slightly above level to screw in the legs—about the length of three full threads; add this amount to the calculated length of pipe legs.

In order to have a place to fasten the hinges to the wall, you may want to nail 2 by 4 or 2 by 6 rails, on edge, between the studs. Sheets of ¼-inch plywood across the rails and studs will give the hinges even firmer backing.

When you fasten the hinges in place, make sure the bench is level and that the legs are securely screwed in place.

In order to keep small tools handy, yet off the bench, the drawing illustrates a simple method for wall storage above the platform: ¾ by 1½-inch oak strips are

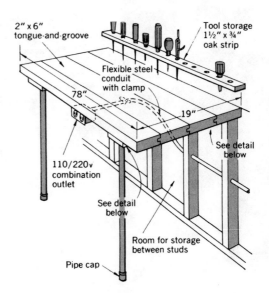

Bench *in working position. For good working surface, nail and glue piece of tempered hardboard to platform.*

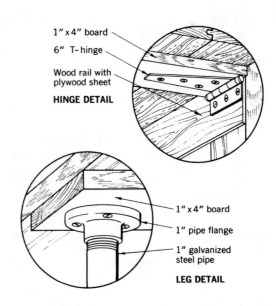

Mounting Details. *Lubricate pipe threads so that the two legs can be easily attached and removed.*

screwed short side to the wall, and a row of holes of various diameters, spaced one inch from the wall, are bored through the wide side to hold items like screwdrivers, chisels, and bits.

Design: William A. McGinnis.

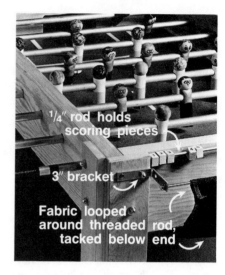

¼" rod holds scoring pieces

3" bracket

Fabric looped around threaded rod, tacked below end

Close-Up *shows details of table.*

Table Soccer *offers rousing fun for from two to eight players. (See color photograph on back cover.)*

Table soccer—a lively game

"Block! Kick it! Goal!" These are the whoops and shouts you'll hear rising from a group gathered around this regulation-size table soccer game. Table soccer is played just like its real-life counterpart—soccer—and it's bound to generate the same unbounded enthusiasm.

Two to eight people can play; it's easy. Just drop the ball on the center mark and maneuver your players to kick the ball into the opposing team's goal and to block your opponents' kicks.

Most of the game's parts can be purchased in raw form at a home-improvement center. Those that can't are not hard to find. The handgrips, made for tricycles, come from a bike shop. Buy the ⅞ to 1-inch-diameter hard rubber ball at a toy store and the fabric or netting for the goal at a fabric shop.

Pick up acrylic paints (for the players' uniforms and the playing field lines) and press-on numbers (for the scoring cubes) at an art store. For the opposing teams, choose uniform colors that are easy to tell apart.

The table is simply a wooden box on four legs. The box's sides are 2 by 8's, glued and screwed together at the corners. The bottom is a piece of ⅛-inch tempered hardboard, resting on 1 by 2's around the perimeter. Two 1-by-2 supports, spaced underneath the field, keep it from sagging. Each leg is made from two 35½-inch lengths of 1 by 3, joined at right angles to a piece of heavy-duty ¾-inch right-angle aluminum molding. So they can be removed easily for storage, the legs are bolted to the box. Appliance levelers attached to a block that is screwed to the base of each leg make the table's level adjustable.

Be sure you have all materials on hand before beginning construction. Cut the box's sides and ends to size, drill eight 13/16-inch holes in each side as indicated, and cut out the goals. Nail the 1-by-2 moldings in place, sloping them up at the corners as shown in the side view. (This will prevent the ball from rolling out of play.) Join the four sides, countersinking two 3" screws in each corner.

Cut the playing field to size and paint on the field markings as illustrated. All lines are ½ inch wide. Using a ruler, first draw them with a pencil, then outline them with masking tape. Apply white paint carefully, removing the tape when the paint is tacky.

While the paint dries, make the legs. For each leg, cut two 1 by 3's to length and join them to the aluminum molding as shown in the exploded view, using contact cement and a few small screws for strength. Glue and screw 1½-inch by 2½-inch-square blocks for the leg levelers to the base of each leg; then add the leveler (drill a hole in the center of each block).

Mark the tops of the legs for bolt holes as indicated in the drilling detail. Then, one at a time, hold them in place—flush to the table's top edge—and drill ¼-inch holes through both leg and box. Push a 2½-inch by ¼-inch carriage bolt through each hole from inside immediately after drilling it, and cap the bolt with a washer and acorn nut.

Before mounting legs on one end, cut ¾-inch by ¾-inch by ⅝-inch blocks and drill a 5/16-inch hole through them for scoring, or use round wooden beads. Thread 10 of them onto a ¼-inch aluminum rod and insert the rod into ¼-inch holes drilled into the edges of the legs as shown in the photo. Mount legs as described below. Add press-on numbers to the blocks or beads.

Sand all wood but don't scratch the aluminum. Then apply a coat of polyurethane varnish (or paint) to the box and the legs.

While the main part of the table dries, you can make all of the players. As illustrated, each is made from a 1¼-inch wooden cabinet knob attached with a 2-inch double-ended screw to a 1-inch-diameter, 3¾-inch-long hardwood dowel. You'll probably need a drill press for drilling the ¾-inch hole that is centered exactly 3 inches up from the base of each dowel. Paint on the uniforms and faces. When paint is dry, completely coat each head and body with polyurethane varnish.

Using a tubing cutter or hacksaw, cut the ¾-inch tubing to 4-foot lengths. You'll need eight 4-foot poles. File the cut edges smooth.

When the table is dry, set the playing surface in place on the 1 by 2's, securing it from above with lengths of ¼-inch quarter round molding along the long sides (use brads). Thread one of the aluminum poles through a side hole, through all of the players designated to it (be sure they face the right direction), and through the opposite side hole. Repeat this with the rest of the poles.

Next, fasten the players to the poles. Here's how. Center a pole and mark exact positions of players on it,

according to the circles on the playing-field sketch. Run a double-ended screw partway into the base of the head that's designated for the first body. Then, holding the body firmly in position on the pole, drill a starter hole down through the center of the dowel's top and through the tube.

Turn the head onto the body until firmly in place. If it balks, don't force it. Instead, drill a slightly larger hole. When you go on to the next player on the same pole, be sure to hold secured players against a block to keep them straight up and down. This is important.

Slide a rubber plumbing washer with a ¾-inch hole onto each end of each pole; then add handles and ¾-inch rubber furniture-leg tips as specified. The plumbing washers, combined with five or six windings of electrician's tape, provide "stops" that keep the players from bashing into the sides of the box. These stops also limit the range of the goalie.

Make each goal from two 3-inch L-brackets, a ¼-inch threaded rod, two acorn nuts, and fabric or netting. Attach the framework as shown in the photo closeup. Loop the fabric over the rod and tack it to the underside of the table.

Design: Donald W. Vandervort.

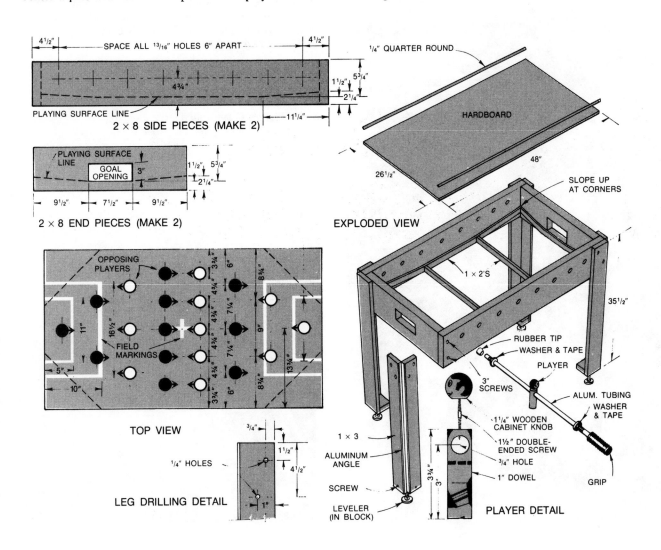

Backgammon board is easy to make

Played for high stakes in European casinos and for fun in American living rooms, backgammon is one of the most popular board games in the world. Hundreds of styles of backgammon boards are on the market, but you can make your own easily and inexpensively. Just preview the following directions, buy the playing pieces and board materials, and assemble everything.

Before buying the board materials, choose your playing pieces (checkers work well); their size will determine board dimensions. You can get checkers or similar pieces at a toy store—buy 30 (15 each of two colors), four dice, and two dice cups. Next, read the directions for laying out the board and then work out the proper board and frame size.

Next, buy the board materials. From a lumber dealer, get a sheet of fine-textured cork for the playing surface, a small piece of ¼-inch plywood for the base, and a strip of wood for the middle bar. At an art store, pick up two broad-tipped waterproof felt markers (one red, one black), a can of clear protective spray, contact cement,

a small roll of felt, and an unfinished wooden picture frame. If you prefer to build your own frame, see helpful construction hints on pages 54 and 55.

Here's how to mark the cork board. The base of each triangle is the width of one playing piece, and the length is that of five playing pieces. Place a strip of masking tape lengthwise across the cork at the height of the triangles (see photo) and mark 24 top points and the center "bar" on it. (The bar should be at least as wide as one playing piece; its variable width can help in making the board fit a premade frame.) Using a ruler and felt pens, draw and color in the triangles (two coats may be needed). Let ink dry, remove tape, and spray on two coats of clear protective sealer.

Place your frame on the cork and mark around the outside edges with a pencil. Then carefully cut along the lines with a mat knife and back the cork sheet with plywood cut to the same size. Measure and cut the bar to length, sand the frame and bar, and apply a protective finish to both.

Finally, glue and brad the playing surface to the back of the frame. Attach the bar with contact cement. After you cover the bottom of the plywood with felt (attach with contact cement), shake the dice and play away!

Design: Diana Bunce.

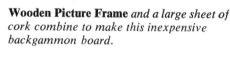

Wooden Picture Frame *and a large sheet of cork combine to make this inexpensive backgammon board.*

Mark *top points of triangles on tape, pencil triangles on the cork, and ink them in with a marker.*

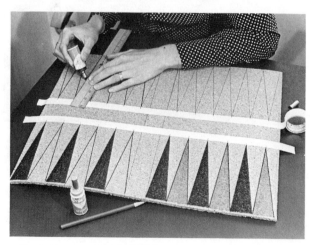

Revolving Cribbage Board *scores up to three players or teams.*

Cribbage action moves clockwise

On this circular, rotating cribbage board, your scoring peg is always right in front of you, no matter where you sit. Twice around completes a game.

To make the board, mark the center of a piece of hardwood that is cut to a 12-inch-diameter disk. Use a compass to mark the rows. The large drawing below shows how to arrange the holes around the board's circumference in degrees. Detail A shows how much space to allow between holes, reading from the center to the outer edge.

Groove the rows with a wood burner. Using a pencil, protractor, and straightedge, mark the scoring peg holes. Drill these holes about ⅜ inch deep; their diameter should be the same as the pegs' diameter. Then drill a hole through the center just wide enough to allow a 1¾-inch-long bolt to turn freely.

The scoring board rotates above a 9-inch plywood disk. Locate the center of the disk and drill a hole for the central bolt (see Detail B). On the bottom of the

disk, recess an area around the central hole large enough to accept the nut, washer, and bolt. Glue felt to the bottom, assemble, and stain or oil.

Design: Robert Huffstetter.

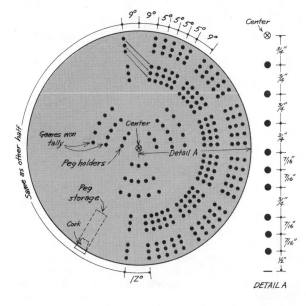

Side View *illustrates how a 1¾-inch-long bolt goes through the center; washers prevent wobbling.*

Top View *shows spacing between peg holes and general layout of the board. Pegs are short wooden dowels.*

Basket Can Be Raised *to regulation height, is held in place by turning latches to a horizontal position.*

Low-Level Basket *provides a reachable target for a pint-sized player; it rests on bottom post braces.*

Adjustable-height basketball backboard

Basketball players of any stature can use this adjustable-height basket. An additional feature: The backboard is 30 inches out from the posts, so the goal affords more than usual playing room.

The backboard is held at the height you want by a pair of latches on the posts. At the lowest level, it's held by the lower brace of the posts (set this at a good practice height for your smallest son). A pair of latches at the regulation 10-foot height and intermediate pairs accommodate players of other sizes.

The materials you will need are listed on the oppo-

site page. In addition you will need a regulation basket and net and some waterproof glue.

MOUNTING THE BACKBOARD

Build the framework for the basket support first, nailing and gluing the braces as shown in the sketch. The two horizontal 1 by 2-inch braces at the rear are the last to go in place, but drill the holes so these braces are ready to mount.

Unless you buy a pre-cut backboard, saw your plywood to the standard fan shape. Drill the holes for the

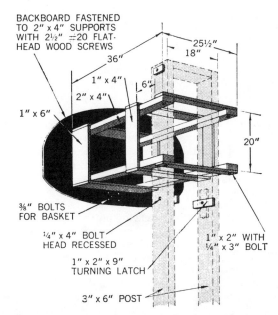

Drawing *shows assembly of sliding framework for backboard, support posts, and latches seen from the rear.*

basket mounting bolts and the holes for screwing the backboard to its supports. Be sure to countersink so the screws fit flush with the surface of the backboard. Mount the basket to the backboard and the backboard to its supports.

ASSEMBLING THE FRAME

Dig two holes 18 inches apart and 3 feet deep (use longer posts if you need to go deeper). With the 5½-inch lag screws, attach stop blocks to outside of posts and fasten top brace. Determine the lowest basket height you want and nail bottom brace to posts at this level. Fasten 1 by 2 by 9-inch latches to inside of each post at the 10-foot height. Sink heads of bolts below surface of outside of each post to permit basket to slide past. Place washers between latch and post so latch will turn easily.

You may need some help to place the posts in the ground. See that they are set at the right depth, and check plumb with a level. Then fill the holes and tamp.

You'll also need help to hoist the basket-backboard assembly into place. Slide the backboard supports onto the posts just above the bottom brace. Bolt the two 1 by 2 by 25½-inch back braces into place. Then bring out the basketball.

ADJUSTING THE HEIGHT

To raise the basket to full height, just place a 6-foot step ladder under the backboard support and walk up the ladder, sliding the basket up as you go. When you get to the top, turn the latches at the 10-foot level to a horizontal position and let the basket settle in place.

Reverse the procedure to lower the basket. Climb the ladder, raise the basket so you can turn the latches to a vertical position, and then let the basket slide down to the supports at whatever lower level you want.

Design: Richard E. Londgren.

Close-Up *of backboard frame at lowest position. Note how the backboard projects from the posts.*

A small portable loom

This little loom is easy to make and allows you to try the art of weaving inexpensively. Unlike most other looms it is easily stored away when not in use. But it's not just a beginner's toy. You can do very professional-looking work on it and you can make larger items by hand-sewing or crocheting swatches together.

Make the frame of 1 by 2 stock. Use ¼ by 1½-inch bolts with wing nuts to attach the legs and heddle arms. The heddle's dowel is simply held on its arms by two rubber bands. There are three holes (three positions) for the heddle arms on the sides. They let you move the heddle upward as your weaving progresses.

Drive ¾-inch 16-gauge brass escutcheon pins, spaced ¼ inch apart, across both the top and bottom of the frame. You'll need 45 per end. Leave about ⁵⁄₁₆ inch of the pins exposed.

Slant the ends of the shed stick on a long taper. For the shuttle, simply wrap a length of yarn or a little stick about the size of the one a drive-in gives you for stirring your coffee.

You can find good books on weaving at your public library, and reading one will not only give you instruc-tions but also an insight into the many varieties of weaving you can do on this loom.

Design: Bridge Mountain Foundation.

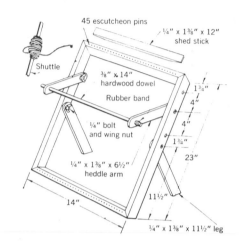

45 escutcheon pins

¼" x 1⅜" x 12" shed stick

Shuttle

⅜" x 14" hardwood dowel

Rubber band

¼" bolt and wing nut

¼" x 1⅜" x 6½" heddle arm

1¾"

4"

4"

1¾"

23"

14"

11½"

¼" x 1⅜" x 11½" leg

Simple Loom *can be set up anywhere, folds flat for storing away, takes almost any material.*

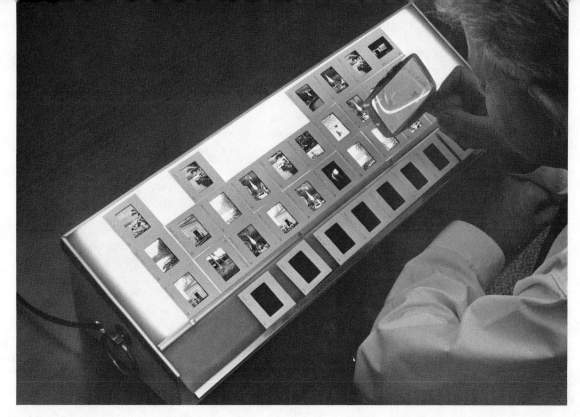

Edit and Arrange *your color slides on this easy-to-make light box. "Reject" shelf is below.*

Light box for previewing color slides

Here's a fluorescent light box that will help you sort and edit color slides. Color rendition is approximately the same as that of your projector. The top of the box accepts three dozen 35-mm slides and lets you view 2¼-inch-square or 4 by 5-inch transparencies and film strips as well. An extension of the top provides a shelf for rejected slides.

Portable, the box is easily carried by a handle at one end; the cord stuffs inside for storage.

To make the light box, first obtain a standard 2-foot, 20-watt fluorescent light fixture with a white or cool-white tube from a hardware or lighting store. (You could use a different length tube and build the box to fit the fixture's length.) Drill vent holes in the back and bottom of the box; paint the inside white.

Use a piece of ⅛-inch, smooth, white translucent acrylic plastic for the top. Secure the top with aluminum counter-edge molding at back and sides. Bolt on a ¼-inch, quarter round aluminum molding for the ledge at the front edge of the lighted area; attach any thin molding along the outer front edge. Mask side edges and the "reject" shelf on the underside with black tape. Install the light fixture, with the switch mounted through the box and fixture. Attach small rubber feet under the box.

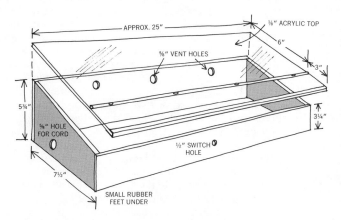

Construct *box's back, bottom, and front from ¼-inch plywood; ends are of ½-inch stock. Small light switch is located on the front.*

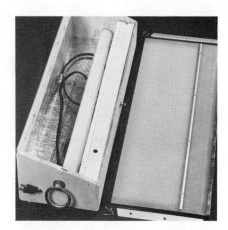

Light Fixture *parts are all readily available. Ring at end is for carrying.*

Large Mosaic *made of new and old chiseled mill ends, boards, dowels goes nicely in garden setting.*

Make these mosaics from mill ends

Weathered Cubes, *some end-on and some exposing chis-eled sides, are used for simple composition.*

Mosaic panels like these are fun to make. The natural textures and colors of the wood go well together, and look their best as decoration for a garden wall or corner.

Collect wooden odds and ends at lumberyards, along the beach, around old houses—wherever you can find an abandoned fragment of wood stock you like. Saw the pieces to a fairly even thickness (small discrepancies add interest), then arrange them in various patterns.

When you are satisfied with a pattern, cut a piece of hardboard big enough to hold the pattern, and a frame of 1 by 2-inch stock. After gluing and nailing the frame, transfer the pieces to the hardboard, fixing them in place with waterproof glue (recommended: resorcin resin or casein). Except in the block panel at lower left, the pieces are joined only to the backing. This allows spacing leeway for odd sizes. You can leave the panels untreated to weather naturally, or coat them with a clear exterior finish.

Design: Doris Aller.

Dowels form a wine rack

To build this wine rack, you'll need two sizes of dowels, white glue, and a means of drilling accurate and true holes. A ⅜-inch brad-point drill bit and a drill press or a portable drill and drill press attachment will work best.

Buy about 12 feet each of ⅜-inch and 1¼-inch doweling. Cut the ⅜-inch doweling so that you have 16 pieces 3⅝ inches long and 6 pieces 12 inches long. Cut the 1¼-inch doweling into 12 pieces 11 inches long. Lightly sand all parts.

Make the three horizontal levels first. For each level, drill ⅜-inch holes halfway through the ends of two of the 11-inch dowels and all the way through the other two. (To avoid break-out problems, drill from one side until the bit point protrudes; then turn and complete the hole from the opposite side.) Insert two 12-inch dowels, working glue into the joints. Make sure the three levels are identical in size and shape.

Drill ½-inch-deep holes for the vertical dowels into both sides of one unit and into one side of each of the other two.

Begin final assembly, using glue to insure rigidity. In-sert eight dowels into the bottom unit, pressing the middle level over these. With a steel square, check for right angles. Let the glue dry. Insert the remaining dowels into the middle unit, press the top unit over, and check again for right angles. For a natural finish, apply Danish oil.

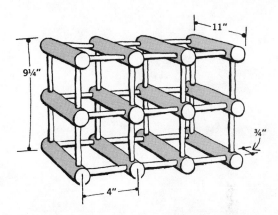

Wine Rack *is easily made, using only a drill and a saw. (See color photo on front cover.)*

To Assemble *a picture frame this way, glue the frame corners together, lay all on a flat surface, stretch a nylon cord taut around the clamping blocks, and tie the cord to a round-head screw.*

A handy jig for assembling picture frames

One way to make picture frames is to use lengths of picture molding available at lumberyards and picture framing shops (or stock lumber) and tailor each frame to the size needed.

With a miter box and a sharp saw, cutting the corners to a precise 45° is usually no problem; but without special clamps you can run into complications when you try to glue the frame together. The pieces keep slipping out of line. Using brads or nails to hold them may not work—nails often split thin frames, and driving them into just-glued miter joints may throw everything out of square.

One solution is to make this inexpensive clamp that adjusts to fit almost any size of picture frame. It stores away in much less space than most commercial versions, yet exerts ample pressure to ensure tightly glued joints. With it you do not need nails at all, although you may want to drive a small brad through each corner for extra strength after the glue has set.

To make the clamp, drill holes through the centers of four 3½-inch blocks and saw one corner out of each block. Groove the two long edges to form a channel for the cord, and add a wood screw as shown in the sketch.

Use ⅛-inch nylon traverse cord. Its smoothness allows it to slide around the four corners to equalize the tension, and its elasticity gives good pressure on the joints. Tie a loop in one end of the cord and burn its ends to prevent unraveling.

Set your glued picture frame on a flat surface, attach and tighten the clamps, and leave it untouched until the glue has set.

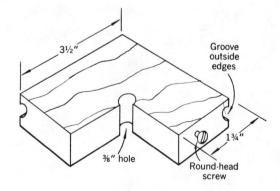

Make Corner Blocks *of ¾-inch or thicker hardwood or plywood. Holes at centers let uneven joints fit snugly.*

An easy-to-make picture frame

This picture frame is easy to make on two counts: You use standard 1⁵⁄₁₆ by 1⁵⁄₁₆-inch corner bead molding, and simply add 1¾ inches to the dimensions of the picture to determine the length of the frame pieces. This kind of frame is fine for any picture requiring mat and glass.

If the matted picture is not already backed, back it with mat board. Run strips of 1½-inch-wide cellophane or cloth tape along the edges of the glass, with 1¼ inches protruding. Turn taped side down, clean the exposed surface, and set the picture and backing face down on the glass. Fold up the tape and, keeping it tight, press it to the backing to seal the picture in a dustproof unit.

Cut four frame pieces to the dimensions of the matted picture plus 1¾ inches. Miter and join. Cut corner L's and ⅜-inch strips from scraps; glue in. Finish the frame as you wish.

Wood Joiners *in corners pull edges together (trim prongs down if too long).*

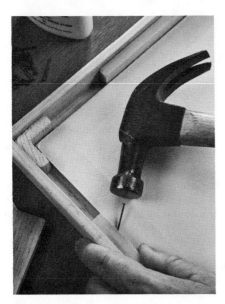

Glue Side Strips *and corner L's in place. Position print, secure with brads.*

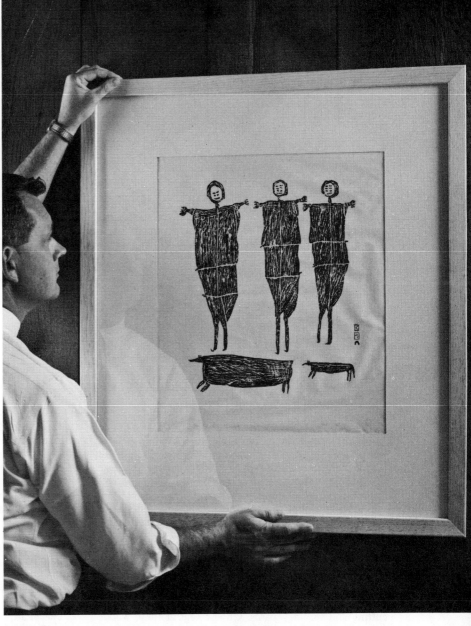

To Hang, *screw eye-screws into frame sides one-third down from top and far enough in from back edge so that frame can hang flush.*

Five Useful Boards *are made from different woods. From top: Walnut square makes a luncheon board; teak disks make small servers or coasters; birch meat board with sloping center is reversible; pine cheese paddle only takes soft cutting; oak breadboard (6½" by 20½") catches crumbs below grill.*

Six wooden cutting and serving boards

A well-designed serving board can make the cook's job easier and be worthy of any table. As a cutting surface, wood is hard to beat. Its warm color and rich grain complement food in all types of dining situations. Some of the boards shown here are simple slabs, sanded and oiled; others require cutting and gluing.

Choice of wood is important in making a serviceable board. In general, most commonly available softwoods make good cheese boards (such as the one with the handle in the group photograph) or serving boards on which only light cutting is done. Pine is best; it splinters less than redwood or fir. Cedar may be too aromatic.

Most of the widely available hardwoods—oak, birch, maple, ash, walnut, teak, even mahogany—make suitable cutting and serving boards. Choose one of these woods if the board must withstand forceful slicing or sawing. (Mahogany scars more readily than the others from

forceful cutting.) Some people feel that teak imparts a distinctive aroma to foods.

The board should be designed to do at least one job— cutting or serving—particularly well, and its size and weight should be scaled for its intended use. You don't want a board so large it will crowd the serving or dining area (although ample working room on its surface is important) or one so heavy it will be awkward to move when laden with a 20-pound turkey. Nor do you want a board so small it overflows with crumbs or juices.

The large meat board with the sloping center section measures about 11 by 17½ inches—it is ideal for a 5-pound roast but skimpy for big cuts. Its large juice reservoir is an important feature not found in many commercial boards.

The oak breadboard's grill insert lets crumbs fall through to the tray below. The grill needs careful mea-

Cut *½-inch-wide, ⅜-inch-deep notches in ¾-inch wood for breadboard grill. Space notches ½ inch apart in short pieces, 1½ inches apart in long pieces.*

Tap *notched grill together with hammer after ripping wood to ½-inch-wide strips and cutting those strips to length.*

Meat Board's *sloping center is joined with waterproof glue and clamped between end pieces. Ends and sides are 1¾ inches high; center is 16 inches long, beveled 2.5 degrees at each end.*

suring and sawing (see photo); the tray's four mitered sides frame an ⅛-inch-thick plywood bottom.

The other three boards in the group picture are simply different types of wood cut to attractive sizes and shapes to make a soup-and-sandwich platter, bar coasters, and a cheese paddle.

If you need a good, lightweight serving board, try an artist's drawing board like the one pictured above. Such a drawing board serves as an extra-wide, prelaminated, solid-wood panel, unique since most finished lumber can be bought no wider than 12 inches.

It's easy to finish the boards, but now and then they may need rejuvenating. After sanding the wood to as smooth a finish as you can, wipe on several coats of mineral oil, allowing each coat to soak in before applying the next. As the boards dry out or become marred, sand them smooth and reapply mineral oil.

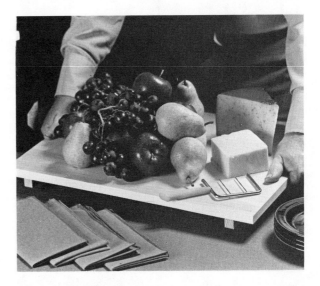

Artist's Drawing Board *becomes generous cheese board. Screw strips of 1 by 1 to bottom for base.*

A cutting block with cutlery shelves

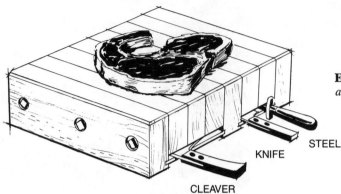

Eight Pieces *of hard maple are glued and bolted to make this cutting block.*

STEEL

KNIFE

CLEAVER

Fish, fowl, or meat can be trimmed, cut, or tenderized on this sturdy butcher block. It is made of eight pieces of hard maple, glued and clamped together with the end grain on top. The pieces are 12 inches long, 1½ inches wide, making a 12-inch square. The block stands three inches high. The side view drawing below shows how pieces are cut to provide shelves for cleaver, knife, and sharpening steel.

Here is how the block is cut and assembled: Cut the two end pieces (A). Drill $\frac{5}{16}$-inch holes for the bolts. Make counter bores so that bolt heads and nuts may be countersunk. Notch the $\frac{5}{16}$-inch groove for the shelves with your power saw dado. If you do not have a dado, make enough cuts with a regular blade to make a $\frac{5}{16}$-inch groove.

Cut the center piece (B) and notch $\frac{5}{16}$-inch grooves on both sides. Drill the holes for the bolts. Then cut the five pieces (C) which go above the shelves and drill the holes for the bolts. For the shelves, cut the pieces from $\frac{5}{16}$-inch-thick maple stock.

Finish the individual pieces as nearly to size as possible. Glue them together with casein glue. Put $\frac{5}{16}$-inch bolts through the holes drilled for them; bolt length should be 11¾ inches. Place the shelves in position. Tighten the bolts to clamp all pieces together. Mill or plane the top surface until smooth and bevel or round off the top edges. Do not oil or paint the finished block; leave the wood natural.

If maple is not readily available, other hardwoods can be used. Also, if your workshop does not have power equipment for making the grooves, for planing the top smooth, and for sawing the pieces to size, ask a local lumberyard to do this work. You can assemble the pieces at home.

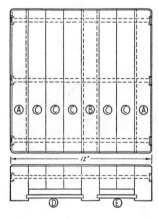

Top and Side *show cut pieces for lower shelves.*

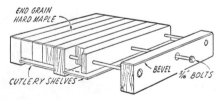

Maple Sections *are 12 inches long, 1½ inches wide.*

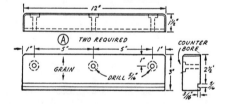

End Pieces *are cut first, holes for bolts drilled.*

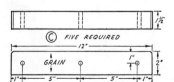

Pieces Above Shelves *are 1½ inches wide, 2 inches deep.*

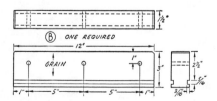

Center Piece *is cut; grooves are notched.*

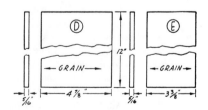

Shelves *are cut from 5/16-inch-thick maple stock.*

This cutting board fits the sink

This 1½-inch-thick cutting board is made from a laminated maple chopping block bought at a lumberyard. Cut to fit the sink, the block is heavy enough that it won't jiggle or move around in use. The top side is hollowed; the resulting edge all around keeps refractory pieces of celery and the like from getting away. Because of the curve on one side, the sink and faucet can still be used with the board in place.

The hole in the board has several functions: Parings go through it and into the disposer. A measuring cup set down in it receives small amounts of chopped ingredients; or a bowl underneath it receives larger amounts. And it's a drain when you wash off the board.

You can duplicate this cutting board if you have a router, shaper, or drill press and router bits (it's almost impossible to hollow out the top of a hard, glued-up maple board with hand chisels).

Make the dimensions of the board fit your particular sink, and locate the hole over or near the disposer. The diameter of the hole will depend on the measuring cup you are most likely to use there (probably the ½-cup size).

Cut the rabbets in the three sides with a router, shaper, drill press, or circular saw. The curved edge is best cut with a band saw or saber saw, but can be done with hand tools. After sanding smooth, finish the board with a generous coating of salad oil or paraffin oil.

Design: Mrs. Suzanne D. Barrymore.

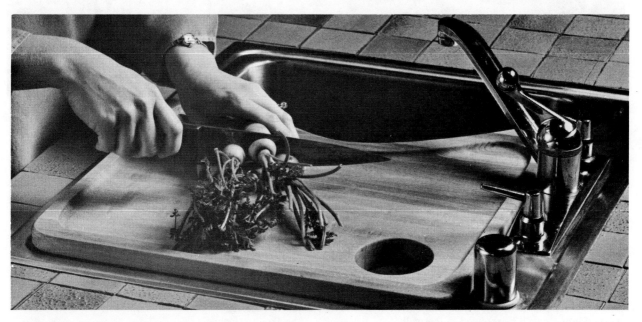

Shaped Maple Board *nestles snugly into sink opening; measuring cup fits into 3-inch hole at right.*

Cut Out *hollow first, with router, shaper, or drill press.*

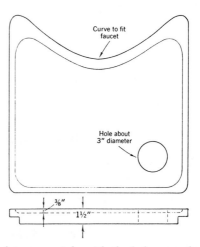

Curve to fit faucet

Hole about 3" diameter

⅜"

1½"

Fit *board to your sink, with the hole near the disposer.*

Thirty-Two Spice Jars *revolve inside this cabinet. To use one, just unscrew it from its lid.*

Spice jars revolve inside this cabinet

One mark of a good cook used to be the spice chest in her kitchen. Here is a modern version which performs some of the same functions as the old—it protects delicate spices from light and is easy to take along if you have to move.

The 2-foot-long chest holds four rows of spice jars, eight jars in each, on a wooden bar that revolves to bring any row within convenient view and reach. Here it rests on a countertop underneath a wall-hung kitchen cabinet. It could equally well be screwed to the wall.

You can build the box of any softwood or hardwood ½-inch plywood with the front trim of matching solid wood. The doors can be of either ¾-inch plywood or solid wood, and they can be cut to be mounted flush or half-lapped (as shown in the photograph).

Center the two small wood brackets for the bar inside the ends of the box. Attach each jar lid to the bar with two small screws. Mark and position each lid so that the jar it receives when screwed in, will have its label to the front.

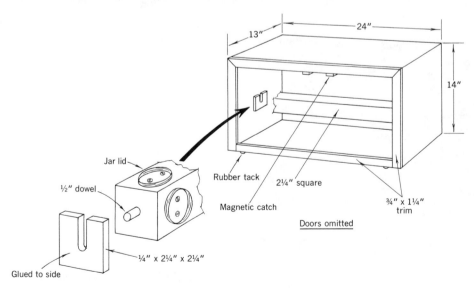

Use a carving gouge for this fruit platter

Here is a fruit platter that you can make with scraps of redwood plank 2 inches thick and 6 to 12 inches square.

Draw out the pattern on a paper folded twice. Saw it out with a scroll saw, or power band saw, jigsaw, or saber saw. Hollow out the inside by cutting across grain with a carving gouge, leaving a flat border of uncarved wood about ¼ inch wide on the outside outline.

When you get the desired depth of the bowl, smooth the rough cross-grain cuts by cutting with the grain. Smooth sides and bottom thoroughly with sandpaper, but rub lightly on the inside, to keep the charm of the many tool cuts.

Rub the bowl with beeswax and polish with a soft cloth.

Carved Platter *is made of redwood plank 2 inches thick.*

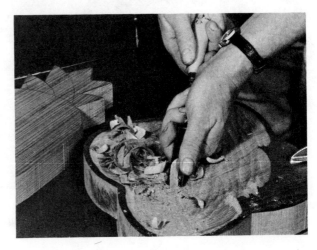

Scoop Out *inside with large gouge, cutting across grain.*

A cutting board and knife rack

Maple is a most durable wood, highly suitable for a cutting board and knife rack. Small painted circles, on filler over the recessed screws, add a decorative touch. Set on its runners, the cutting board also can be used for buffet service of breads, cold meats, and cheese.

On a piece of paper, make an outline of the design you would like. Trace this pattern onto a 1 or 2-inch piece of finished stock. Use a coping saw, jigsaw, or saber saw to cut around the outline. With a drill, make the hole for hanging and smooth off rough edges with a wood rasp. Then sandpaper for a smooth finish.

The lower runner strip is grooved to catch knife tips (see diagram below). Insert the screws through the runners, leaving the cutting side smooth.

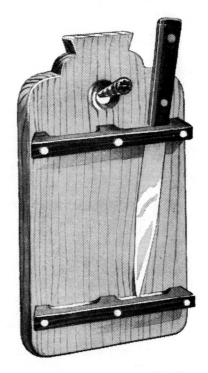

Lower Runner Strip *is grooved to catch knife tips.*

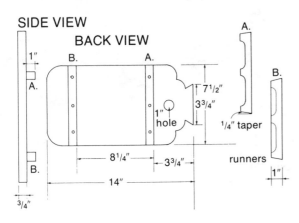

SIDE VIEW

BACK VIEW

A.

B.   A.

1"

A.

B.

7½"

3¾"

1" hole

¼" taper

B.

8¼"   3¾"

runners

1"

14"

¾"

Fruit Tray *is made from an 18-inch piece of 3 by 10-inch Douglas fir. Cracks and knot add to old wood effect, are accentuated by flame and steel wool process. Finish with varnish or lacquer.*

Wood-flamed trays and bowls

For all their distinctive character, the pieces shown here are made of one of the most common of West Coast woods, Douglas fir. The emphatic graining is the result of burning out the soft summer growth by controlled flaming and leaving the winter rings elevated. Since Douglas fir has these hard winter rings, it is an especially satisfactory wood to work with.

To make fruit and nut bowls, candlesticks, trivets, and trays by this wood-flaming technique, choose the piece of wood by the suitability of its grain structure. For a large object, use wood with widely separated winter rings; for smaller pieces use wood with closer grain.

Rough out the wood in the general shape of the object you are making; chisel or rout larger depressions and smaller gouges where desired. The flaming process will accentuate cuts in the surface of the wood, so keep them smaller than you want them to be on the finished article.

To flame the wood, use a blowtorch or a propane hand torch. Play the torch over the wood until it has caught fire, the flame subsides, and you see a deep red glow. To keep from overburning one spot, work over areas of about 4 square inches at a time.

When the piece is completely charred, brush off the char carefully with a wire brush, following the grain pattern and using a light touch so that the soft layers will not be unduly scratched. Polish with steel wool until all shiny char is removed; begin with coarse wool, finish with fine.

If the wood is extremely dry, a single burning may be enough; usually, however, two or three rounds of flaming and polishing will bring out the grain better.

A coating of varnish or lacquer darkens the wood but produces the most durable surface. If you prefer a dull finish, you can apply two or three coats of good paste wax to the finished piece.

Nut Bowl and Trivets *made by flaming process. Trivets show enlarged saw cuts for added design interest.*

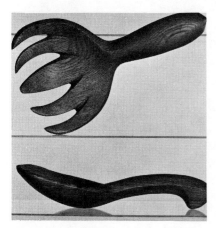

Curve *across bottom and top of handle stops at sharp edge on each side.*

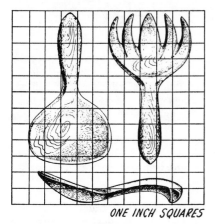

ONE INCH SQUARES

Spoon, Fork *are identical in size. Cut the tines with a saw or knife.*

Hardwood Salad Set *is in scale with large salad bowl. Tines of fork are cut with saw or knife and filed out with wood file or rasp.*

You can hand carve this salad set

If a salad bowl is used frequently at your table, you may want this handsome serving set. You can carve one for yourself with little difficulty.

A band saw will simplify the first cutting job considerably. However, if you are willing to give more time to the job, you can do all rough shaping of the set with an ordinary coping saw and wood rasp.

Use any good hardwood so that your set will not splinter or break. Oak, mahogany, or maple will be satisfactory. For interesting grain and pattern, you might try orchard wood if you can find large enough pieces.

If you are not accustomed to working with hardwood, make a trial run on pine or fir. On the soft wood, you'll be able to work out any kinks in production. Try to copy the dimensions accurately. A variation in shape or size wouldn't be serious, but these proportions work very well.

The pieces of wood should be at least 2 inches by 5½ inches by 9½ inches. Knots or blemishes, so long as they are not loose or soft, will add to the appearance, but might make cutting and shaping more difficult, particularly if you do not have power tools.

Lay out the design on the flat side and then on the edge or profile side. If you use a band saw, cut the edge side first on both pieces. Clamp or otherwise hold the waste back in place temporarily while you cut around the flat side.

If you use a coping saw, reverse the procedure. Cut the flat side first. On the profile side, use the saw only around the handle, down to where it joins the bowl. Use a wood rasp or chisel to complete the profile around the bowl.

Shape the spoon and fork with a rasp or piece of glass used as a scraper. Cut the tines with saw or knife and file out with a wood file or rasp. Sand with coarse, then fine paper to get a smooth finish.

For deep color and long life, rub with hot olive or salad oil. Constant use in your salad bowl will keep the set in good condition.

Four-Foot-Long *candelabra can be rearranged into virtually any configuration.*

Knobs and dowels form a candelabra

Spread it out, push it into a star shape, or break it into shorter sections—this candelabra can be arranged any way that suits your needs.

You'll need about 9 feet of 7/16-inch hardwood doweling and thirty-three 1¾-inch hardwood knobs; they're sold at hardware and lumber stores and home improvement centers as drawer knobs (with small flattened spots) or as parts of shelving systems (full rounds).

To build the candelabra, you'll need a drill press or an electric drill in a drill stand, a 7/16-inch twist bit, a 1-inch bit, and a saw.

Prepare to drill the holes by first making a jig from a scrap of wood, drilling two 1-inch holes about 3 inches apart. Center one jig hole under the bit. Position knobs in the jig to drill holes for candles and vertical posts. In 19 knobs drill all the way through, using the 7/16-inch bit; in 14, drill only halfway through.

To insure the correct drilling angle for side holes, use a 2½-inch-long dowel to link two knobs through vertical holes; then set knobs two at a time in the jig holes as shown in the small photograph. Drill side holes halfway through all knobs except 7 of the 19 that have holes drilled completely through (these 7 become the top knobs).

Cut 13 dowels 5 inches long for the horizontal bridges, 12 dowels 1½ inches long for the short vertical posts, 7 more at various lengths from 2½ to 5 inches long for the upper vertical posts.

Sand dowel ends if necessary to fit into the holes. If dowels are too loose, dip ends into water so they will swell slightly. Do not glue. The finished candelabra can be oiled, painted, stained, or left natural.

The 14 narrow candles (or tapers) are more easily fitted into the holes if you first dip their bases in warm water to soften the wax.

Design: Peter Schait.

Squeezed Together, *this 14-candle holder is easy to store. Next time it's needed, use all of it or part of it—whichever you choose.*

Drill Holes Straight *by setting the linked knobs in a two-hole jig.*

Potpourri box displays collectables

Collections of almost anything—seashells, pine cones, dolls, dried flowers, or forgotten items buried in drawers —can become objects of art when attractively arranged under glass in decorative display cases.

You can begin this display box using an inexpensive, small, wooden picture frame and glass purchased at a variety store. Or build a frame yourself from mitered framing stock and buy single-thickness window glass.

Cut out the ¼-inch plywood backing board to fit the frame; then cut the 2¼ by ¼-inch lath sides to make a simple butt joint as shown in the drawing.

Smaller wooden laths form the partitions; fasten them to the back with small brads or glue. When using a purchased frame, you'll have to notch the laths where they touch the frame's outside edges so the glass will rest directly on the inner partitions of the wall box.

Finally, the display box may be painted, stained, or finished naturally.

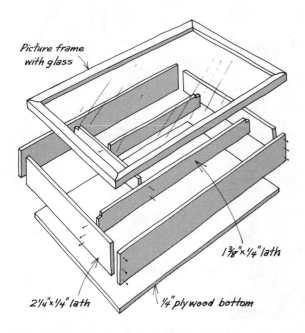

Seashells and Gravel *become esthetically interesting when organized in a display box.*

Glue and Brad *glass frame to face of box after cutting partitions. Picture wire on the back is best for hanging.*

Wide Variety *of collectables and memorabilia can serve to give display boxes a theme.*

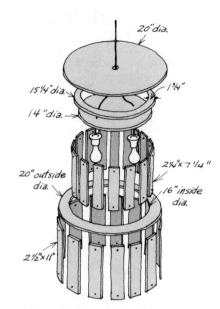

20"dia.

15¼"dia.

14"dia.

1¾"

2¼"x7¼"

20"outside dia.

16"inside dia.

2½"x11"

Exploded Diagram *shows how the battens and the rings interrelate.*

Dowels and Glue *hold this circular ceiling fixture together.*

Board-and-batten ceiling light

Leftover redwood batten inspired the design for this attractive hanging light fixture. Light shines between the offset battens, showing off the fixture's contours.

To make the wooden frame, you'll need 28 feet of redwood batten, a 3 by 4-foot piece of ½-inch plywood, and 6 feet of 3/16-inch dowel. Cut parts to size as shown in the diagram: 16 battens 11 inches long, 16 more 7¼ inches long (trim these to 2¼ inches wide), two disks, and two rings.

Using a protractor, mark the outside edges of the top disk and ring and the bottom ring every 22½°. Mark the inside of the bottom ring at the same intervals but offset these marks to fall between the marks on the outer edge.

At each mark, drill a 3/16-inch-diameter hole ½ inch deep for dowels. (For proper drilling alignment, start holes with a small nail.) Drill 3/16-inch holes 2 inches in from both ends of each long batten. In each shorter batten, drill a 3/16-inch hole ¼ inch from the top, and another hole ¾ inch from the bottom. Drill a ⅜-inch hole through the center of the top disk for the main

fixture wire; in the 14-inch disk, drill two holes 3 inches from the edge (along a diameter line) for the light socket wires.

Connect the bulb receptacles—simple porcelain sockets costing about $1 each will do; consult electrical suppliers for proper wire size and assembly. Screw the receptacles to the 14-inch disk, the wires protruding through the two holes.

Glue the top ring to the top disk, offsetting the ring so that the holes fall midway between those on the disk. Slip the fixture wire through the disk hole and attach a strain relief clamp to it. Connect the receptacle wires to the fixture wires. Fasten the 14-inch disk to the top ring with wood screws.

With dowels and wood glue, secure the short battens to the outside of the top ring and the inside of the bottom ring. Secure the longer battens to the outsides of the top disk and bottom ring.

Try 25-watt bulbs for general use, 50 to 75-watt bulbs for reading areas.

Design: Malcolm George and Charles Hanf.

Spotlights *for highlighting or reading clamp anywhere along the shelves' edges.*

Shade and Block *have enough weight to hold lamp in position. The cord can run over or under the shelf, then behind it.*

Reading light grips a shelf

Gravity keeps these lamps in place along bookshelves. The lamps have notched hardwood blocks that slip onto ¾-inch shelves at any point and pivoting brass arms that angle the light in the desired direction. The weight of the blocks keeps the lamps firmly in place.

Three pieces of walnut glued together and notched make the base of each lamp. Cut the notch just a fraction of an inch wider than your shelf's thickness. Drill a ⅜-inch hole through the center of the block to house the threaded brass nipple. Attach nipple with epoxy glue. Cut a shallow groove for the cord inside the notch as shown in the drawing. Run the cord through the groove and either above or below the shelf. You can buy the brass shade (made to hold a large glass lamp shade) and all of the other electrical hardware at an electrical supply store. Use a low wattage (50 to 75 watt) spotlight bulb.

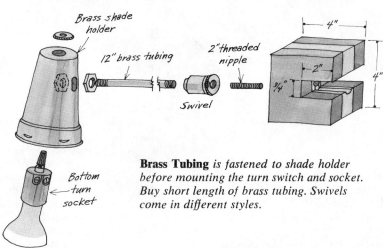

Brass Tubing *is fastened to shade holder before mounting the turn switch and socket. Buy short length of brass tubing. Swivels come in different styles.*

Buy the works, make the clock

Many clock shops carry a variety of clock works and accessories around which you can design and build a clock. You may buy inexpensive, battery-powered works for about $10 or more expensive, wind-up movements for $20 to $75. When properly adjusted, good battery movements—those with at least seven jewels—will operate accurately for two years on a single battery. Wind-up movements in the $35 to $75 range will, with occasional cleaning, give years of accurate service.

You should buy the movement before designing the clock because the size, shape, pendulum clearance, and method of mounting will determine design possibilities.

You'll find a variety of clock hands, faces, and numerals at well-stocked clock shops. Stationery stores, sign shops, and craft shops are other sources of materials that might make good clock fittings.

Once you have the works, you can use the ideas on this page or rely on your own imagination to come up with a variety of unusual housings.

Clock Housings *are custom made. Small clock is run by battery power; pendulum clocks wind up.*

Glass-Fronted *redwood box houses attractive 30-day movement with chimes. Designer felt numerals weren't needed. Design: Peter O. Whiteley.*

Electric Movement *powers this clock. Chisel out a 1⅜-inch-deep hole in the back to receive the works. Design: Rick Morrall.*

Teak Arch *and cylinder cover eight-day wind-up movement. Arch is series of ¾-inch-thick arches glued together. Brass rods hold center cylinder; hardwood dowels mark numerals on ⅜-inch-thick faceplate. (See color photograph on front cover.) Design: Norman A. Plate.*

Wheelbarrow *holds almost ½ yard of soil or leaves when sides are in place.*

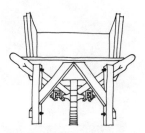

Rear View. *Note bolts and wheel supports.*

Removable Sides *make moving bulky items an easy job.*

New day for the wooden wheelbarrow

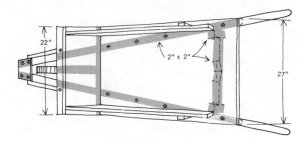

Side View. *Use galvanized 5/16-inch bolts on the frame. Adjust clearance of frame to fit your wheel.*

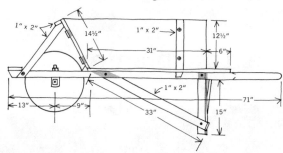

Top View. *Frame is 2 by 2's with 1 by 2 supports. Front, sides, and floor are ⅝-inch exterior plywood.*

Wooden wheelbarrows, widely used a few decades ago, have some distinct advantages over the more modern metal-tub type. You can't mix concrete in them, but they're better for moving large objects and, when their removable sides are in place, they can carry more bulk.

To build one, first obtain a wheel and determine how much clearance it needs in the frame. The wheel shown is a steel-rimmed one at least 30 years old. Ball bearing wheels with pneumatic tires are less picturesque but easier to find, and they roll better on soft or bumpy ground.

Assemble the wood frame to fit your wheel, using screws and 5/16-inch carriage bolts; glue all joints. Fashion the two axle supports from short pieces of heavy channel iron or angle iron.

The exterior plywood sides are held in place by two 1 by 2 stakes near the rear (as shown) that extend down through holes cut in the exterior plywood floor and by two 1 by 2's on each side that slide into two pairs of holes cut in the front.

Round off the handles with a coarse wood rasp, sand the wood, and treat it with a protective finish.

Design: Ralph P. Olsson.

Rough and Finished Redwood *was used to make these four large planter boxes, but any western softwood will work equally as well. Drill five ¾-inch holes through the bottom of each box for drainage.*

Every garden can use a big planter

A big plant container can play a special role in the garden. In an entry, or at one end of a deck, or in a patio, it can become a striking landscaping element. In it can go a single shrub or small tree, as well as annuals for year-around color.

The four large wood containers shown above are inexpensive and quite easy to make. The two with grooved designs (1 and 3) are of rough-cut 2-inch redwood. To make the grooves, you will need either a table saw, with dado blade, or a router. The container with vertical boards (4) is of finished redwood, except you can use rough lumber for the bottom. On a table or radial-arm saw, rabbet 4 by 4 corners to the thickness of the finished 2 by 4's. Use galvanized nails throughout (and on all the other boxes). If the nails tend to protrude through this finished lumber, drive them at an angle, which will also make them hold better.

For further instructions on how to make each container see the diagrams on the opposite page.

Use a Wire Wheel *with an electric drill to accent grain and to subdue weather stains in all rough-cut lumber.*

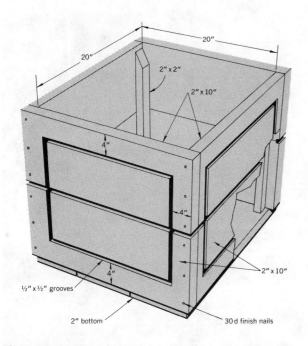

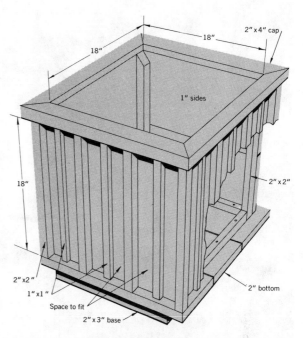

1. Build this big container (the same as number 3), by stacking 2 by 10's for the sides, adding 2 by 2's on the inside corners. Besides the rectangular design, rout or dado the joint between the two rough-cut 2 by 10's of each side to obscure it. Seal joints or line the interior (and those of the other boxes) with polyethylene plastic sheeting to prevent seepage.

2. You can construct this container as a simple box, then add the vertical outside trim and the 2 by 4 cap. Use finished lumber throughout. Assemble the base first, then nail on the 2 by 2 inner supports and the 1-inch sides. Then drive the nails for the vertical trim from the inside, so they will not show. Use both glue and nails to hold the mitered joints of the cap together.

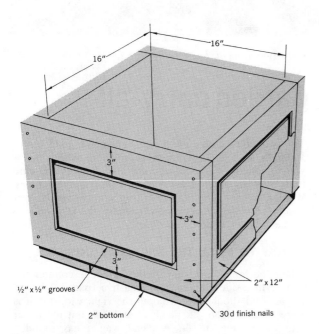

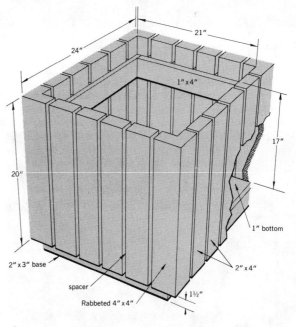

3. Two sides of this container butt over the others—usual box construction. Sides sit on a 2-inch bottom which is cut slightly short on all sides to give extra height and dimension. Seal bottom joints with emulsified asphalt or glue; use long thin, galvanized or cement coated nails for maximum holding power without splitting. Rout or dado and chisel out rectangular design.

4. To build this container, first assemble the bottom, then nail and glue on the four rabbeted 4 by 4 corner posts, then the four 1 by 4 upper rails. Equally space four 2 by 4's between corner posts on each side. Since 2 by 4's vary in width, measure the openings left between, and cut 1-inch lumber to fit. Use finished lumber, except for the bottom piece.

Wagon Bed *serves as a storage shelf for barbecue cart. Top contains two hibachi; has serving area.*

Barbecue cart or garden carry-all

Hopper *with canvas sides and bottom transforms wagon into handy cart for leaves and lawn clippings.*

The two units shown on these pages make good use of a child's wagon. Its large, easily-turning wheels allow you to roll the barbecue counter anywhere in the yard that you wish, and to store it under shelter at other times. When you have quantities of leaves or clippings to carry away, the wagon becomes a carrier for the large canvas hopper shown at left.

HOW TO MAKE THE BARBECUE COUNTER

Adapt the long dimension of the barbecue counter for a loose fit inside your wagon. The five spaced 2 by 2's at each end should give it about the right width; if it is more than ½ inch off, notch in or block out the lower ends of the legs to fit. A metal wagon has rounded corners; if you are using one, cut off the four corner legs at the height of the wagon sides so those legs will fit over the corners.

The width of redwood 2 by 2's may vary as much as ⅛ inch in different mill runs, so for uniformity, buy all the pieces you need at one time. When assembling the base, secure the pieces with glue and use only one nail

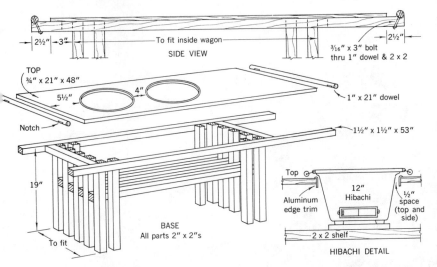

SIDE VIEW

2½" 3" To fit inside wagon 2½"

³⁄₁₆" x 3" bolt thru 1" dowel & 2 x 2

TOP
¾" x 21" x 48"

5½" 4"

Notch

1" x 21" dowel

1½" x 1½" x 53"

19"

To fit

BASE
All parts 2" x 2's

Top

Aluminum edge trim

12" Hibachi

½" space (top and side)

2 x 2 shelf

HIBACHI DETAIL

Barbecue Counter. *Make the base of redwood 2 by 2's; make top of ¾-inch closet shelving. Position the shelf at height to fit your hibachi.*

Counter Lifts Out *of wagon easily; needs no bolting down or support.*

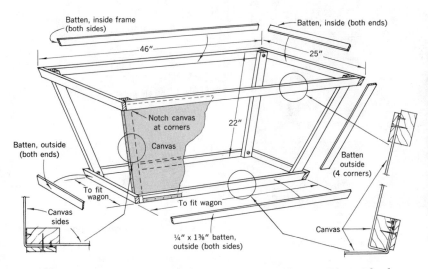

Batten, inside frame (both sides)

Batten, inside (both ends)

46"

25"

Notch canvas at corners

Canvas

22"

Batten, outside (both ends)

Batten outside (4 corners)

To fit wagon

To fit wagon

Canvas sides

Canvas

¼" x 1⅜" batten, outside (both sides)

Leaf Hopper. *Make the frame of 1 by 2's. Assemble two sides with glue and screws in each corner, then glue and nail on the end pieces.*

Lightweight, *the large hopper is easily emptied or placed in a car.*

at each joint (to avoid splitting the ends of the 2 by 2's).

You can use ¾-inch plywood for the top, but a "glued-up" ¾-inch pine or fir board is more attractive here. Available at most lumberyards, these wide boards (used for shelving) resemble huge breadboards and are made of several narrow boards edge-glued together. They cost about the same as plywood.

Cut holes in the top to fit your hibachi, and trim their edges with aluminum linoleum molding to reflect heat. After the top is attached, secure some pins or small wood blocks on the shelf to prevent the two hibachi from sliding about when you move the cart.

Notch the two hardwood dowel handles to fit flat on the 2 by 2 rails, and slant their bolts as shown.

HOW TO MAKE THE LEAF HOPPER

You can cut its angled 1 by 2 frame members quite easily with a hand saw. Temporarily assemble the two long

sides first, as shown in the drawings, and check to see that they will fit inside the wagon (with space left for the ¼-inch battens). Cut these 1 by 2's extra long so they will extend out at the corners. After gluing and screwing them together, trim off their ends with your handsaw at the angles the frames form.

Next, glue and nail two extra-long 1 by 2's to each end, then saw off the excess at the angles formed.

To fit inside some automobiles, the height and length of the hopper may have to be reduced.

Cut the battens (12 required) to fit the frame. If you intend to paint the wood, do it now before the canvas is added.

Use heavy 24-inch-wide canvas. Tack or staple it to the longer sides first, notching it at the corners and stretching it around 1 by 2's where shown. Then cover the two ends. Attach the bottom canvas last, and nail on the battens (use copper boat nails). If you expect to carry wood and rocks in the hopper, substitute a piece of ¼-inch plywood for the bottom canvas.

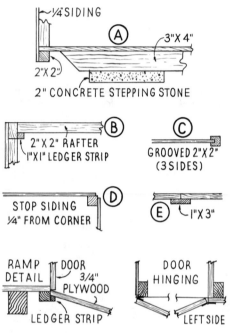

Four Doors *of this storage shed open wide—everything is accessible. Raised floor helps keep shed dry, has ramp (right) for wheelbarrow, mower.*

Details. *Use waterproof glue and galvanized nails when assembling.*

An all-purpose garden storage unit

This freestanding storage shed can go anywhere in your yard that complies with your local building regulations. You may consider placing it against the house or garage, or using it as a screen for one end of the patio. Since it rests on two sturdy skids, it can be easily moved. It keeps garden supplies and tools where they're needed and has room for storing camping equipment, outdoor furniture, and games. It also has a potting counter.

Height of the shed can vary a foot or more to fit a fence or wall—just keep a 6-inch slant on the roof. You build the floor first, using exterior plywood (as elsewhere), nailing it to the two redwood skids and trimming it underneath on all four sides with 2 by 2's. Each skid rests just above ground on three concrete stepping stones. Before positioning, turn the floor upside down and give it a coat of paint.

If you wish, you can "prefab" the two sides and back, nailing studs and crosspieces to the ¼-inch hardboard

siding before erecting. Nail the siding to the 2 by 2's underneath the floor to lock all in place.

A 9-foot 2 by 3 roof beam and two central 2 by 3 studs frame the entire front. The two 2 by 2's shown are the only rafters needed. Install the cabinet partitions. Then nail the 2 by 2 trim (detail C) to the two ends and front of the roof panel, including seam compound in the trim's groove. The 4 by 10-foot panel of asbestos-cement board required can be ordered through any lumberyard, is weatherproof, and (being one piece) eliminates laps and leaks.

Slide the roof in place and secure to all four sides and two rafters with a dozen large-head roofing nails. Drill pilot holes through the asbestos and place a dab of sealing compound under each nail before hammering down. Avoid extra holes through the roof—there's no need to nail the cabinet partitions to it.

The four doors are of ¾-inch plywood, cut to fit.

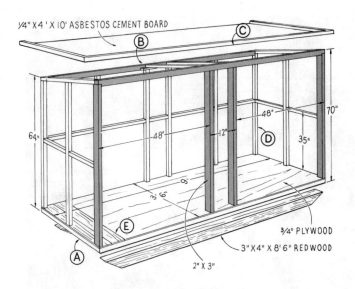

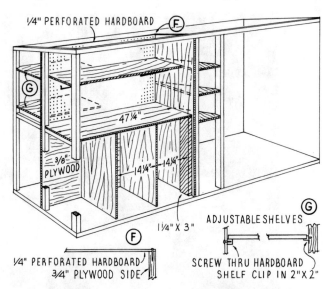

Shaded Frame Members *are 2 by 3's; others are 2 by 2's. Use 4 by 8-foot plywood panel for floor and "E" pieces.*

Interior Partitions *and shelves are installed before attaching roof. All those not specified are ¾-inch plywood.*

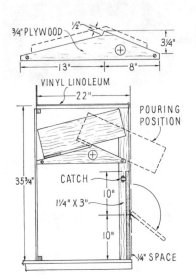

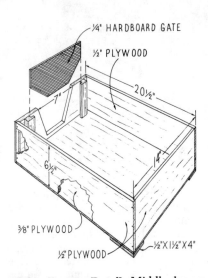

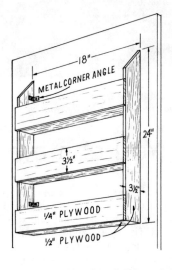

Potting Counter Cross-section. *Use waterproof mastic to secure linoleum.*

Tilting Drawer Detail. *Middle drawer is same size without "gate," rear stops.*

Door Shelves. *Build others the same, except 3½ feet in height.*

Hang each with four 2 inch butt hinges to eliminate warpage and carry the weight of loaded door shelves. Locate tops of the doors 1½ inches below the roof to clear its 2 by 2 trim (add a ¾-inch thick strip there after hanging).

Although not shown, the hinges of one of the left pair of doors are inside; those of the other door are outside. (The doors on the right side are hinged the same, in reverse.) The two doors at left extend down to cover the 2 by 2 floor trim; the two at right are shorter to clear the ramp.

When hanging the sets of door shelves, screw the metal corner angles to the shelving first, slightly in from the back edge, then screw to the doors, thus pulling the shelves tight against the doors. Four corner angles are ample to secure each set.

So that the hinged upper half of the bin front will clear the shed's door, the two bin front pieces butt against not over, the 1¼ by 3 upright on the bin's right side.

Cut the three cabinet drawer fronts from ¾-inch plywood and rabbet them as shown on both sides and bottom. Slanting the gates of the two tilting drawers at the bottom helps prevent clogging when filled with fertilizers. Two of the tilting drawer slides screw to uprights instead of resting flat against cabinet partitions; glue pieces of ¼-inch plywood to their sides to keep drawers from moving sideways (see potting counter detail).

Your drawers may vary slightly from the 14-inch width given. Size them to fit quite loosely in the partition spaces. The middle drawer simply slides on two 1 by 2's fastened to the bin partitions there. Cut a shallow hand pull in the top of its front.

Two Small Kegs, *5-gallon size, are both legs and planter tubs for this patio coffee table. Table top is eight 5-foot redwood 2 by 2's, spaced ½ inch apart, glued together, then cut out for barrels to slip in.*

You can make a lot of things out of barrels

Look closely at the curves and joinery of a wooden barrel and you marvel at its construction. Evolved through the ages, the barrel has unusual strength, tightness, and mobility (its shape allows it to be rolled about easily). Its shape is also handsome. For that reason, especially, homeowners can put wooden barrels to many more uses than just holding liquids.

If you follow the simple procedures described here, transforming wooden barrels into the objects shown on these pages (or into other things you may have in mind) will be easy and fun.

Before you cut a barrel into two tubs, drill holes through each metal band and secure the bands with screws. Otherwise the band may drop off while you are cutting, letting the staves spread, or it may part from the staves when they dry out and shrink.

Use No. 6 or 8 pan-head sheet metal screws or round-head wood screws. If you are going to use the tub as a planter, four equally-spaced screws in the band nearest the cut edge are usually enough; the moisture of the soil keeps the wood from drying out, and the weight will help hold the staves in place. Bands on objects that will dry out between uses should be secured more firmly. If you are making the large ice bucket shown on the opposite page, use a screw on each stave at the upper band. For a smoke oven, put a screw in each stave on each band.

If you are going to cut the barrel in half lengthwise again put a screw into each stave at each barrel band. Even if you are going to use the barrel whole, as for a see-saw, it's a good idea to fasten each band with two or three screws.

The drawing on the opposite page shows how to cut barrel to get two tubs with handles. For tubs without handles, you can cut along both sides of the bung hole, or glue the bung in place and make one cut centered through it.

A saber saw cuts a barrel easily. A handsaw requires a little effort, but will cut a 50-gallon barrel in two in about 15 minutes. After sawing through a few staves, finish the job with the end of your handsaw inside the barrel, to cut more easily across the grain.

Planter tubs will last longer if you coat the inside with asphalt paint; fir tubs especially need this protection. Paraffin-lined barrels do not need the paint.

Drill three or four drainage holes (about ½ inch each) through the bottom of any planter tub.

The exercise wheel (see opposite page) uses very simple bearings. You drill a 1½-inch hole through the center of each end of a barrel and screw a 1½-inch pipe deck flange over each of these holes. A 1¼-inch pipe (the axle) will slip through the two 1½-inch deck flanges, which serve as the bearings. Drill a hole through the 1¼-inch pipe just outside of each flange and place cotter keys in these holes to keep the barrel in place.

Exercise Wheel *is used 50-gallon barrel on pipe axle between tree and post. Bar above is adjustable.*

Half *of a 15-gallon oak keg makes this party-sized ice chest for chilling beverages in ice. It preserves ice well.*

Saber Saw *with coarse blade is an excellent tool for cutting barrel in half; a handsaw will also work.*

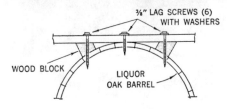

Barrel See-Saw *is 50-gallon oak barrel on which 11-foot 2 by 12 is secured by blocks and ⅜-inch lag screws.*

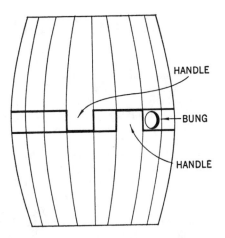

For Tubs with Handles, *cut the barrel as shown here; you waste only the width of the bung hole.*

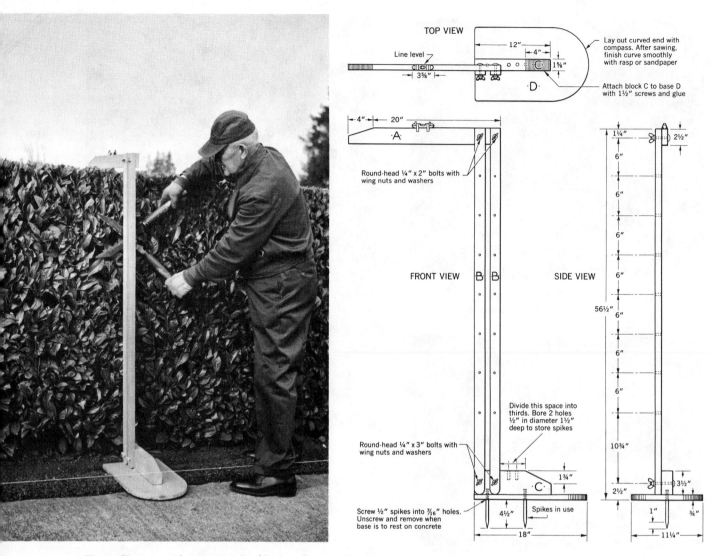

TOP VIEW

Line level

12"
4"
1⅝"
3⅜"

Lay out curved end with compass. After sawing, finish curve smoothly with rasp or sandpaper

Attach block C to base D with 1½" screws and glue

·D·

4"
20"

·A·

Round-head ¼" x 2" bolts with wing nuts and washers

FRONT VIEW   B B   **SIDE VIEW**

1¼"
2½"
6"
6"
6"
6"
56½"   6"
6"
6"
6"
10¾"
2½"

Divide this space into thirds. Bore 2 holes ½" in diameter 1½" deep to store spikes

Round-head ¼" x 3" bolts with wing nuts and washers

·C·   1¾"   3½"

Screw ½" spikes into ⁷⁄₁₆" holes. Unscrew and remove when base is to rest on concrete

4½"   Spikes in use   1"   ¾"

18"   11¼"

Taper Shaper *guides a neat job of hedge clipping. Upright section is set vertically (it could be at any angle). Top piece is always horizontal if ground is level. Base can stand on concrete or soil.*

It helps you clip a hedge straight

Called a "taper-shaper" by the designer, this lightweight gadget is a flexible, adjustable parallelogram with extensions. Placed beside a hedge, it guides clipping for consistent, one-plane surfaces. You can set the upright section straight up-and-down or at any angle. The top remains parallel to the ground and may be set as low as 12 inches above the ground.

Placed on soil with spikes attached (see drawing), the base will hold the uprights at any angle. You just install the spikes and step on the base to push them down into the soil. Without spikes, on a hard surface, counterbalance the base with a bag of sand if you extend the uprights at an extreme angle. For accurate alignment, put a tight guide string lengthwise along the hedge. Set the string so that the nose of the baseblock follows the string as you move the taper-shaper along it.

Design: Everett Scrogin.

Spikes *with threaded ends are inserted into bottom of base for use on soil; remove them for use on concrete.*

This soil sifter is designed to fold up

A collapsible soil sifter can be a handy device for gardeners. It carries the weight of the soil on its own four legs and you supply the sifting motion by shifting or rocking the top from side to side.

The sifter is made of ¾-inch pine in lengths and widths shown in the drawings below. First cut the two ends of the box and make the 4-inch hand slots. Then nail the ends to the sides. Attach the ¼-inch galvanized hardware-cloth screen to the bottom as shown.

The legs are 30 inches long, putting the sifter box at table height. To install the legs, clamp their tops to line up flush with the ends of the box, then bore four holes through the legs and box to receive round-head 2-inch bolts. Secure the bolts with wing nuts and washers. A coat of paint or enamel will improve the appearance of your sifter.

If you sift outdoors in a high wind, you can spread the bottoms of the legs outward and bring the box close to the ground so the siftings won't blow away.

The sifter is designed to fold up as a compact unit for easy storage.

Design: Everett Scrogin.

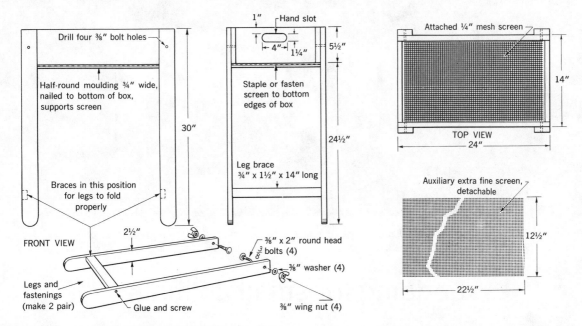

Ready for Work, *the sifter legs are tightened in vertical position. Shovel in dry soil, compost, or sand.*

Hold Sifter Box *by hand-slots, bring legs together, and rock device side to side; fine material sifts through.*

Swimming Pool *for daily baths is attached to deck of house, can be unhooked for emptying and cleaning. The deck provides a clean passageway between house and pool. Succulents are watered from pool splashing.*

Lodging for small animals

Although built for a pet duckling, this elegant but practical duck house could be used to house other animals as well. It is also easy to maintain.

The feed tray is on a removable wall, and a loose nest box simply lies on the screen floor, above ground for easy hosing off. The combination of screened and solid walls gives ventilation, light, and shelter. The deck reduces muddying. The swimming pool easily unhooks and lifts for emptying.

Frame the floor first, except for the outer 1 by 2's on front and left sides. Staple a piece of ¼-inch mesh galvanized hardware cloth (also used elsewhere) across the house floor area, then erect the plywood front and right-side walls.

Cut a matching plywood gable for the left side, and finish the roof framing. Staple wall screening to insides of studs and outsides of beams, notching the wire as needed. Make the screen door and slip it down in place before nailing down the front roof section. Hinge the rear roof and entry ramp with web strapping.

Cut the feed-tray wall to fit—so it can be slipped up (top edge between roof beam and gable) and then dropped down (bottom edge between the two floor beams).

Sliding Screen Door *is locked by wood peg in the floor, to prevent visits by unwanted guests.*

Wall Section *has feed and water tray attached to inside. It easily slips up and out for weekly cleaning.*

Rear Section *of roof hinges up for daily feeding and weekly cleaning with the garden hose.*

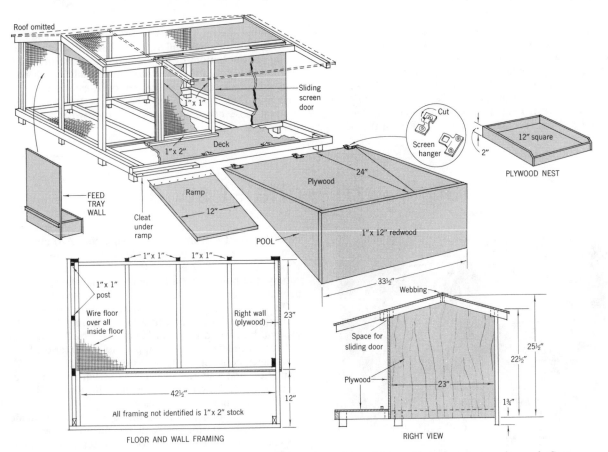

Roof omitted

1" x 1"

Sliding screen door

1" x 2"

Deck

1" x 2"

FEED TRAY WALL

Ramp

12"

Cleat under ramp

POOL

Plywood

24"

1" x 12" redwood

33½"

Cut

Screen hanger

12" square

2"

PLYWOOD NEST

1" x 1"   1" x 1"

1" x 1" post

Wire floor over all inside floor

Right wall (plywood)

23"

42½"

12"

All framing not identified is 1" x 2" stock

FLOOR AND WALL FRAMING

Webbing

Space for sliding door

Plywood

23"

25½"

22½"

1¾"

RIGHT VIEW

Wall, Roof, and Deck *panels can be cut from one 4 by 8-foot sheet of ⅜ or ½-inch exterior plywood. Cut the roof panels 15 by 48 and 25 by 36 inches in size. Use galvanized nails to assemble.*

This rabbit hutch is easy to clean

Front Door *hinges for easy feeding. Two rabbits can live happily here.*

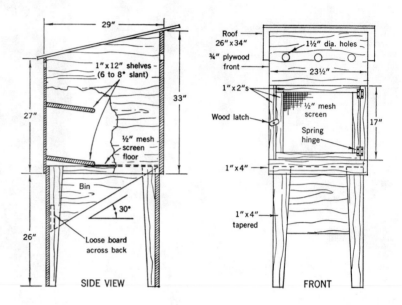

Make *the sides, rear, roof, and the two bin sides of ⅜ or ½-inch exterior plywood. Drill ventilation holes in rear wall near the top.*

If your children become the proud owners of bunnies, a hutch like this one will make caring for them relatively easy. It is not difficult to build, accommodates two rabbits even when they're full-grown, and is simple to keep clean.

The construction details are shown at right. Make the sides, rear, roof, and the two bin sides of ⅜ or ½-inch exterior plywood. Drill three 1½-inch-diameter ventilation holes in the rear wall near the top. Round the edges of the two shelves (rabbits like to chew), and slant the shelves so droppings will roll off. Use galvanized sheet metal for the bottom of the slanted bin. Make the bin to fit loosely between the four legs, and attach it with bolts and wing nuts so it can be removed periodically for cleaning. The rear side of the bin is left open; you place a loose board there between the two legs to hold droppings.

Dog house—chalet style

Insulated Walls *give this dog's outdoor home more than enough winter comfort. Materials are inexpensive.*

A ski chalet for a dog? That's what this A-frame dog house resembles. Simple to build, the structure is rainproof and rests above ground to avoid dampness. Though roomy, the house is small enough and insulated enough to make a dog's body heat create interior warmth.

To plan the size of the house, measure your dog's turning radius. Then construct an A-frame from 2 by 2's, nail hardboard to the inside of the 2 by 2's, and nail redwood benderboard, overlapped, to the exterior. Stuff newspaper between the hardboard and benderboard for insulation and cap the exterior peak with a length of sheet metal flashing to keep out the rain. Redwood 1 by 4's hold the benderboard in place.

The 30 by 36-inch floor in this dog house was made from ⅜-inch exterior plywood resting on rot-resistant, redwood 2 by 2's. Cover the floor with scraps of indoor-outdoor carpet.

Design: Pat von Merveldt.

Open at Both Ends, *this sturdy feeder has brass welding rods to keep out large predatory birds.*

An A-frame bird house and feeder

This delightful bird feeder is made of solid mahogany with brass hardware.

You can use lower-cost materials, of course, and change the dimensions as desired to utilize whatever lumber you have on hand. Cut out the roof, bottom, and the two low sides first and assemble these temporarily to ascertain the exact height of your 1 by 1-inch center beam. Notch the two ends of this beam to receive the two upright posts.

A brass welding rod makes good bars for the two ends. Space the bars 1½ to 1¾ inches apart to give entrance only to small birds.

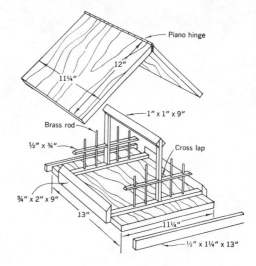

One Side *of the roof hinges up so that feed can be scattered on the floor; this is also handy for cleaning.*

Angled Cuts *are at 45°; dimensions can be changed to make use of scrap lumber. Heavy roof needs no catch.*

For Storage, *remove dowel-tipped legs, close front.*

Fold-Down Front *makes convenient work surface. Pots, small tools, and other garden supplies are stored on the shelves.*

Wall cabinet . . . its face is a table

A wall-hung cabinet with a hinge-down front can store garden equipment and provide a work table for potting and other small jobs. It could just as well hold barbecue equipment and a hibachi.

The 16-inch-deep box can be screwed or nailed to a wooden wall or fence. It has sides, front, back, and shelf made of 1 by 12 and 1 by 4 rough redwood. Three 40-inch-long 1 by 12's nailed together along two 1 by 4 cross braces form the front door-table. A 2 by 4 braces each corner of the box.

The table top, fastened to the cabinet with two strap hinges, is supported by a pair of dowel-tipped legs—the dowels fit into matching holes in the door's cross braces. Folding table leg braces help support the table top. When you want to hide clutter by closing the door, simply pull off the legs (store them on top) and fold up the front.

"Penny Farthing" *bicycle inspired this whirligig. Large wheel is three boards joined by corrugated fasteners.*

Woodsman's Ax *hits stump with a clack when wind turns the paddles around. Exploded drawing of components is shown below.*

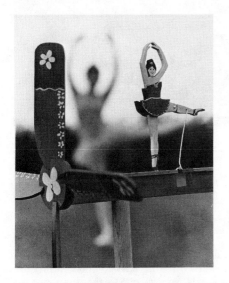

"Pavlova" Ballerina *executes high kicks whenever the wind commands.*

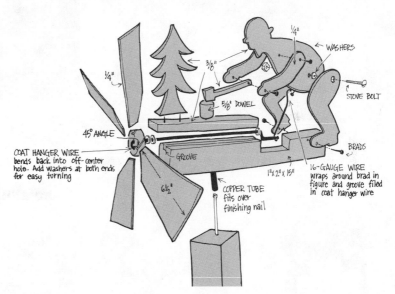

Whirligigs put the wind to work

Whirligigs—folk toys that date back many years—are enjoying a mild revival. In one part of the country, gardeners mount whirligigs on poles, claiming the vibration of the turning windmill drives away moles. Elsewhere, whirligigs are used to startle birds. You can use them to inspire chuckles and add whimsy to your garden.

The whirligig operates only in wind strong enough to spin the windmill blades, which turn the cranklike coat hanger wire that makes the figure bob. The wire is bent and connected to the figure with a length of thinner wire as illustrated. Washers and a lubricant help reduce friction.

The ¼-inch and ⅜-inch pine pieces are cut from door moldings. You can cut out the figures with a band saw, jigsaw, saber saw or coping saw; the groove for the coat hanger wire can be cut with a handsaw or table saw. You will also need a hammer, a drill, and pliers.

Each whirligig has a 2-inch-long copper sleeve that fits tightly into a hole drilled in the bottom of the figure. Ask the hardware dealer to cut this from a piece of copper tubing. Drive a 3-inch finishing nail into the top of a wooden post or fence, mount the sleeve over it, and let the whirligig swing freely to point out the wind's direction.

Simple projects from scrap lumber

Simple tortilla press

This Mexican tortilla press works well and can be easily made from a few scraps of lumber.

For the press itself, use any ¾ to 1-inch-thick wood on hand, choosing unwarped boards that will fit together evenly. Cut the paddle-shaped bottom from an 8½ by 12½-inch piece, leaving a handle on one end where you attach the 2 by 2 pressure arm. Glue and nail four 1 by 2 cross-pieces to the top and bottom boards to help prevent warping when the press is washed.

Last, locate the arm's ¼-inch bolt at a height where the arm can lever down (not completely horizontally) over the top of the press.

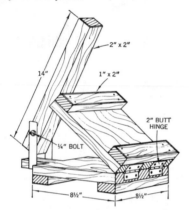

Wooden Press *makes tortillas flat, uniformly shaped.*

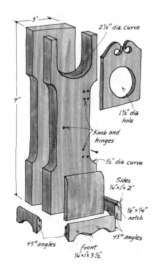

Grandfather watch

Grandfather's old pocket watch often ends up forgotten in a dresser drawer. But this easy-to-make miniature grandfather clock lets you display—and use—one of these classic timepieces.

The watch case is built from layers of walnut. You use a drill to make the large circular cutout for the watch's face and a coping saw to cut the decorative contours at top and bottom. To make the compartment where the watch rests and the curves along the clock's sides, drill holes with appropriate diameters (see drawing); then saw out the wood between the holes to make broad U shapes.

The three pieces that make up the feet are notched along their length and cut at a 45° miter so they fit neatly around the base of the clock.

After all the pieces are joined with plastic resin glue, they are sanded and oiled. Small brass brads simulate a knob and hinges. A square of foam glued in the back of the watch slot holds the timepiece snug.

The dimensions of this "clock" can be changed to fit your particular watch.

Design: William T. Bess.

Teak milk caddy

This project might better be labeled "how to disguise a not-so-beautiful milk carton so it can look attractive on your table."

Actually, these teak milk caddies (which could be made from other woods, as well) have more than esthetic merit. They insulate the carton, keeping milk cold longer, and their handles make pouring—even from the half-gallon size—easy for youngsters.

A caddy should be built to fit snugly. Measure the bottom of the milk carton exactly; then add ⅛ inch to allow for expansion. The height of the box is determined by the height of the carton. To keep weight to a minimum, plane the wood you'll use for the sides and bottom to about ⅜ inch.

Attach the handle (cut from a piece of ¾-inch teak) with glue and reinforcing dowels before gluing the sides and bottom together. Use waterproof resorcinol glue. Hold the box together with a wood vise or clamps while it's drying. After sanding, finish with mineral oil.

Half-Gallon *or quart-sized milk cartons fit snugly into their holders so they stay in place when tilted.*

Long Dowel Handle *balances an off-center load. The length of the saw determines length of tool box.*

Tool box for a beginner

When children reach the age of 8 to 10, they are usually eager to do some woodworking and repairing of playthings by themselves. But they're often discouraged if you give them a child's tool box. Unless it's an expensive kit, the tools it contains are usually so inferior and difficult to use that they can accomplish little with them.

They can do much better with a few real tools and this easy-to-make tool kit. The simple construction of the tool box is shown in the drawing. Assemble it with nails and white glue, and finish with stain wax.

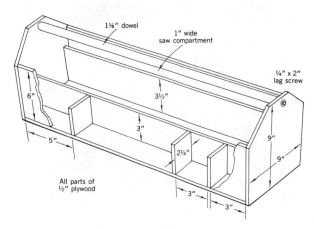

Eighteen *different kinds of hardwood, joined with resin glue and three steel rods, form top of table.*

Odds-and-ends coffee table

The interesting thing about this table is the variety of hardwoods that make its top. As a way to use odds and ends of hardwood lumber, this project can produce striking results.

Construction is simple: Saw the accumulated boards and scraps into 1½-inch strips, and trim to 24 inches in length. Different thicknesses of stock will cause no problem. When the strips are laid together with the 1½-inch sides vertical, they form a uniform slab. Three ⅜-inch holes drilled through each strip (except the two selected for end pieces) accommodate ¼-inch steel rods, threaded on each end (see sketch).

For assembly, coat the strips with phenolic resin glue, and clamp together with nuts tightened onto the threaded rods. Heavy weights on top of the slab while it dries can keep warping to a minimum. Then cut off the ends of the rods flush with the nuts, drill 1-inch holes about ½ inch deep in the end strips to receive the protruding nuts, glue the end strips in place, and clamp.

You can cut the beveled legs from a block of hardwood, or glue up thinner boards to make the necessary bulk. Attach the legs in pairs to oak crosspieces with white glue and two 3½-inch number 12 screws per leg. Leave the two leg units unattached to the table until all finishing is done, then screw them to the bottom with eight 1½-inch number 12 screws each.

The table can be finished any way you like. Here's what was done to this table: A belt sander with very coarse paper leveled off the top, which was then finished with progressively finer grades of paper—down to number 400 wet-or-dry paper—on a felt sanding block. After a coat of sealer, 12 coats of clear polyurethane finish (sanded between coats) completed the table and filled minute gaps between strips. The last coat was hand-rubbed with pumice and paraffin oil, and waxed. Three coats of polyurethane on the underside protect it from expansion or contraction from humidity changes.

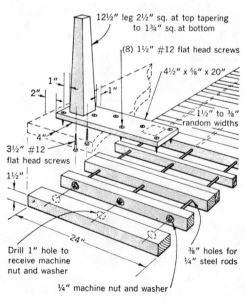

12½" leg 2½" sq. at top tapering to 1¾" sq. at bottom

(8) 1½" #12 flat head screws

4½" x ⅝" x 20"

1"

2"

1"

1½" to ⅜" random widths

4"

3½" #12 flat head screws

1½"

24"

Drill 1" hole to receive machine nut and washer

⅜" holes for ¼" steel rods

¼" machine nut and washer

Table Assembly. *Top is 24 by 54 by 1½ inches; table stands 14⅝ inches high, is strong enough to sit on.*

Low Candleholder *allows talk across the table.*

Tall Stand *holds 13 candles near eye level. Candles sit on 2 by 2's—four 18 inches long and four 30 inches long. Stem is a 5-foot-long 4 by 4 nailed to 18-inch base.*

Five candleholders from scrap lumber

Do recycling and candleholders interest you? This project highlights both, for all the materials for these functional candleholders came from the scraps of other projects. And to get these imaginative results, you don't need any sophisticated tools.

The candleholders on this page were made from standard sizes of vertical-grain Douglas fir. Pieces of 1 by 2, 2 by 2, 2 by 4, and 4 by 4 were cut to the desired lengths and simply glued or nailed together. Nails were countersunk and the resulting holes were plugged with a matching filler.

Careful sanding before gluing or nailing enhances the wood grain and gives the pieces a fine, handcrafted look. Though the candleholders shown here were all left unfinished, they could be stained or painted. Or you could use an entirely different wood.

Whether you make one of the holders shown or design your own, be sure the candle flame is kept away from all wooden surfaces, and don't position your candleholder in a breezy spot.

For best results, buy high-quality candles. Inexpensive candles may tend to burn down quickly, making them uneconomical, or they may burn unevenly, leaving large puddles of wax on the table or floor.

Random Scraps *of 2 by 2, 2 by 4, and 4 by 4 were sanded and glued together in a sculptural form. A variety of candles could be used.*

Hanging Candelabrum, *made from seven pairs of 1 by 2's, graduates by 2-inch increments from top 8-inch lengths to 20-inches at the bottom.*

Outdoor Holder *consists of four 12-inch 2 by 2's at corners and eight 4-inch 2 by 4's in between. Glued pieces are hung with a chain.*

New case for an old clock

This nautically-neat electric clock, with its oak case and brass screws, began life more mundanely as a plastic-and-chrome kitchen wall clock.

Old Clock *once hung on the kitchen wall. It's been given a new look from a case made of oak flooring.*

This case is 8 inches square; you may need to adjust the size to suit your clock mechanism. Glued-together scrap 2-inch by 5/16-inch oak strip flooring, found at a hardwood floor company, forms the front and back. A coping saw was used to cut the face opening.

The clock mechanism was screwed to the back of the case. Then the old face was removed and a new one designed, using dry transfer lettering on mat board (both available in art supply stores). A square sheet of glass protects the face. The case was assembled with flathead brass wood screws countersunk flush; then it was sanded and oiled.

Design: William R. Dutcher.

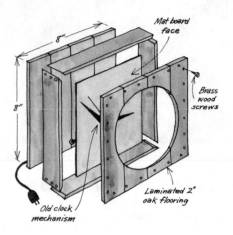

Rack for barbecue tools

This barbecue tool rack keeps everything together and handy for use. And it simply hangs on two hooks. After a barbecue you can take it away from the patio and hang it on a similar pair of hooks on an inside wall of the garage or other protected place. Then your tools stay clean and rust-free and, if hung fairly high, they are out of the reach of small children.

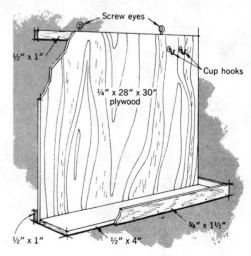

Use Glue *and nails to assemble wood parts. Alter dimensions to fit your barbecue equipment, lumber on hand.*

Movable Rack *holds skewers, tongs, scraper, spatula, fork, spoon, spit motor and rod, salt, pepper shakers.*

Raised cutting board

This cutting board is made of walnut but could just as well be made of inexpensive pine. Cut and attach the legs at a 20° angle, using a waterproof glue in the slots. If you do not have a power saw to cut the slots, attach the legs with deep-set screws through the top. Finish the board with a coating of salad oil, applied with a rag. Attach four small rubber-headed tacks to the bottoms of the legs to serve as bumpers.

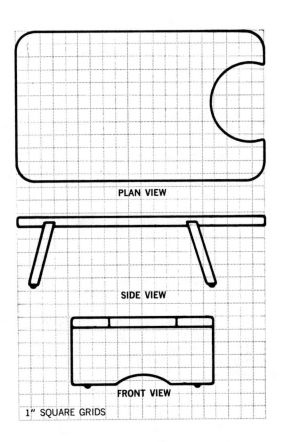

PLAN VIEW

SIDE VIEW

FRONT VIEW

1" SQUARE GRIDS

Walnut Cutting Board *is raised to make it easy to add vegetables at different times to hot pan.*

Dimensions *can be varied. Make legs high enough to clear your favorite salad bowl; round all edges well.*

Three 50-Foot Hoses, *a water timer, and sprinklers are carried by hose cart; holes in handle hold loose hose ends.*

Handy hose cart

To make this hose cart, just cut a 6-foot length of 2 by 2-inch stock exactly in half with a 45° cut. Notch the legs 13 inches down from their tops (squared ends) for a square cross-lap joint (see diagram). Drill the holes for the wheel bolts; glue the legs together. At the midpoint of a 2 by 4-inch piece 4 feet long, cut deep notches to receive the legs. Trim the upper end for a handle; bolt all three pieces together. The 1¼-inch holes below the notches are for loose hose ends; the 1-inch holes hold the nozzles.

Design: Richard E. Londgren.

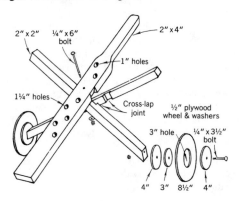

2" x 2"   ¼" x 6" bolt

2" x 4"

1" holes

1¼" holes

Cross-lap joint

½" plywood wheel & washers

3" hole   ¼" x 3½" bolt

4"   3"   8½"   4"

A guide to finishing techniques

Part of the fun of working with wood is choosing a finish that enhances and suits a particular project. The most suitable finish depends on two considerations: how tough a surface you want, and the type of wood you are using. Before using the finish you like on the project, it's a good idea to try it out first on a scrap of the same wood.

PROTECTIVE FINISHES

Most wood must be protected. Left in its natural state, it is too easily soiled or damaged. Wax, shellac, lacquer, varnish, and oil are all transparent protective finishes that help preserve the natural color of wood.

Waxing. Wax gives a soft lustrous gloss but it protects wood only from dirt discoloration. First, apply a thinned coat of shellac or resin sealer. Then sand lightly and follow with at least three coats of paste wax, buffed after each application.

Shellac. Shellac gives a hard, glossy surface, but doesn't provide a very tough coating. It is recommended only for surfaces not subject to hard wear. To apply, thin two parts liquid shellac with one part denatured alcohol, apply with a brush or rag, sand when dry, and wax for protection.

Lacquer. Used a great deal on commercial furniture, primarily because of the speed with which it can be applied, lacquer also offers good surface protection. Application can be either by spraying or brushing. Five or six sprayed coats are usually adequate—any more may crack.

With brush lacquer, you must wait for each coat to dry. Each new coat softens the one beneath; therefore, work fast, keep the brush well loaded, and draw it over the surface only once.

In either case, the final coat should dry at least 48 hours before being sanded or hand rubbed.

Varnish. Generally considered to be the most practical and durable of all transparent finishes, varnish comes in many types and varieties. The gloss varieties usually provide the toughest finishes. If sealer coat is desired, thin the first coat with one part turpentine to six parts varnish, or use a resin sealer. Sand the sealer coat with fine paper or steel wool, and follow with three finish coats. For a dull, hand-rubbed appearance, use either a satin finish varnish for the last coat, or rub the last coat of a gloss finish variety with pumice and oil or water. Any one of several other rubbing compounds on the market, such as rottenstone, will also reduce the gloss and give the finish a richer, velvety appearance.

Oiling. Boiled linseed oil, properly applied, will not only seal wood but provide a durable finish. Apply in thin coats while warm, allowing each coat to dry for 48 hours and rubbing with fine sandpaper between coats. Professionals use 6 to 12 coats.

Newer Danish oils are wiped on with a rag quite easily. Spread a generous coat on the wood, let it stand 1 hour, wipe off the excess, and let dry overnight.

WOOD FILLERS

Many woods have uneven grains and large pores that must be filled if you wish to have a smooth finish. Wood fillers are made of silica or fine sand ground with oil and Japan dryer, or mixed with a hard-drying varnish. If the surface of your project needs a filler, apply it with a stiff brush and work well into the grain. Setting-up is marked by a loss of shine, at which point wipe across the grain with a piece of burlap. Allow the filled surface to harden for 24 hours before giving it a light sanding. (Note: Do not use fillers over a wax finish.)

WOOD STAINS

Wood is stained to emphasize its natural grain. Many professionals use stain only when natural wood has little beauty of color or graining. Stains enhance or change the visual character of wood but give a surface little or no protection. You may want to use a stain first, then protect the surface with one of the finishes mentioned earlier.

Pigment Oil Stains. Similar in many respects to thin paints, pigment oil stains do not penetrate wood deeply and are not light-fast (not immune to fading in sun rays). They may be applied easily with a brush and should be wiped with a clean rag soon after application. The longer you delay wiping, the stronger the color. Let each coat dry at least 24 hours.

Spirit Stains. These stains penetrate extremely well, but are not light-fast. They are difficult to apply because they dry with great speed. Clean rags are the best applicators. Drying time is 15 minutes.

Non-Grain-Raising Stains. These stains combine most of the advantages of other types of stains with few of the disadvantages. They penetrate deeply, are light-fast, dry quickly, and are easy to apply with either brush or rag. Non-grain-raising stains will bleed through finish coats unless sealed with a wash coat of shellac. Drying time is 4 hours.

HOW TO FINISH WOODS

Here are some of the most commonly used woods with suggested finishes for each. With the materials described above and the rules described here, you can work out many finishes of your own.

Walnut. Hard and porous, walnut always requires a filler for a smooth finish. However, if you wish the texture to show, eliminate the filler.

For a natural finish, mix natural wood filler with a little burnt umber. Fill the wood, sand lightly, and finish with two coats of water-white lacquer.

For an antique gray bleached finish, first bleach the wood (use any commercial bleach available for woods), then sand until the natural color shows, then use a gray filler. Finish with a coat of lacquer or varnish.

For a stain finish, apply the stain, fill the surface of the wood with a wood filler that matches the stain, and finish with varnish or lacquer.

Mahogany. There are a number of varieties and grades of mahogany. The most common is Philippine mahogany, which is softer than other varieties, spongy in texture, and large-pored. The finish mahoganies come from the West Indies, or from Central and South America. They range in color from a light claret to a medium dark, pinkish brown. All require a filler for a smooth surface.

Oil or wax produces the best natural finish.

Much modern furniture is made of bleached mahogany. Bleach, wash thoroughly with water, and sand until the natural pink of the wood shows through. Fill with a natural wood filler, and finish with clear lacquer.

Mahogany is stained more often than it is left natural. Apply the stain, fill, and finish with varnish or lacquer.

Oak. Strong and durable, oak has large pores that require two coats of filler for a smooth finish.

A natural finish requires filler and a water-white lacquer finish. To soften the yellow cast, use a slightly gray filler.

Two of the most commonly used stain finishes are golden oak and fumed oak. Golden oak may be achieved by applying golden oak stain, filling with a light brown filler, and finishing with varnish or lacquer. The resulting color will be yellow with dark brown filled grain.

Fumed oak produces an orange-brown color similar to the color in most oak hardwood floors. True fumed oak is produced by exposing the wood to ammonia fumes. No task for an amateur, it can be duplicated by applying Adam brown stain, then a dark brown filler. Sand, then finish with varnish or lacquer.

A similar but darker finish, like early English oak, is obtained by mixing Adam brown with about 1/10th part black stain. Apply a wash coat of shellac, fill with black filler, finish with varnish or lacquer.

For weathered oak, use a light gray stain. Too much will give a bluish cast rather than driftwood gray.

Maple, Birch, Gum. These woods have enough characteristics in common that their finishes may be considered together. Maple and birch are very hard, non-porous woods. Gum is non-porous, but is not as hard. It is usually darker than either maple or birch and must be bleached in order to obtain as light a finish. Maple

and birch are rarely bleached. None of these woods requires a filler.

Any of the natural finishes work well on any of these woods. Gum has less character than either of the other two, and usually is used to imitate some of the more expensive woods.

All of these woods take stains well. You can produce many of the traditional period furniture colors on any of them. Before applying the stain, give these woods a wash coat of shellac, made by thinning one part of white shellac with five parts of alcohol. Then stain and finish with varnish or lacquer.

Pine. About the only soft wood that has a very high value in furniture, pine has a very tough, dark grain and a very soft, light-colored grain. It is a close-grained wood that requires no filler.

To finish pine in a nearly natural color, apply a coat of lacquer sanding sealer, sand thoroughly, and finish with lacquer or varnish.

Pine will take all of the stains that work well on maple, birch, and gum. If you intend to disguise it with a stain, it is a good idea to apply a wash coat of shellac before staining, sand well, stain, apply lacquer sanding sealer, sand, and lacquer.

Teak. Very porous, quite hard, and very durable, teak requires two applications of filler to achieve a glass-smooth finish. If you wish to retain some of the porous texture of the wood, use only one application.

Since teak is about the color of nutmeg, it is rarely bleached. When it becomes wet, fibers of the wood swell, making the surface very rough. To eliminate the possibility of a rough surface finish, sponge the wood with hot water before you apply any finish. Allow the surface to dry, and then sand with No. 7/0 sandpaper. Dust or vacuum thoroughly. Then apply your finish materials.

Never use shellac or any other sealer on teak. The natural oils of the wood are not compatible with shellac gums.

For a natural finish, use water-white lacquer or oil.

The traditional stain finish for teak is black. Apply a stain made up of one part dark walnut stain, one part dark mahogany stain, and one-half part black stain. If the fibers swell in spite of the hot water application, sand and stain it again. Then apply a filler made up of a pint of natural filler, four ounces of lamp black, a half pint of turpentine, an ounce of linseed oil, two ounces of Japan dryer, and an ounce of red color in oil. Highlight by sanding with No. 7/0 sandpaper just enough so that the grain and some of the natural color of the wood shows through. Finish with wax or lacquer.

A WORD OF CAUTION

Many of the projects shown in this book call for a combination of woods—the choicest hardwoods being used in the more conspicuous places, the less costly being used for legs, backs, and framing. For this reason, you'll often have to experiment with finishes in order to produce a uniformly rich appearance.

Some woodworking terms you'll often hear

A-C. One of the most frequently used grades of fir plywood. It has one side of "A" (top grade) and the other with imperfections of "C" grade. Other common grades are A-D, A-A, and shop grade (the poorest).

AIR-DRIED. Any lumber which is seasoned by exposure to the air rather than to artificial heat.

BATTEN. A thin narrow strip of wood used for covering a joint between two boards.

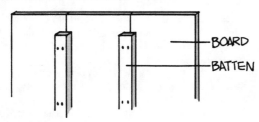

BEADWORK. Ornamental wood molding, usually with a rounded design.

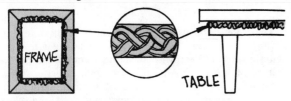

BENCHWORK. Any cabinet work done with hand tools at a workbench, rather than on power machines.

BLEEDING. In wood finishing, the exuding of pitch, a preservative, or a stain through the finish coat.

BLIND DOWEL. Doweling in such a way that the dowels are not visible on the surfaces.

BOARD FEET. A unit of measure for lumber. A board foot is a piece of wood 1 foot square and 1 inch thick.

BOAT NAILS. Any nails with threads or rings to give stronger holding power. Also called screw nails.

BUTT HINGE. Any plain flat hinge, large or small, of the rectangular type commonly used on house doors.

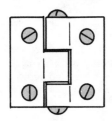

CARBIDE-TIPPED. A cutting tool, such as a circular saw blade, lathe chisel, router bit, or masonry drill, that has hard, long-wearing tungsten-carbide cutting tips.

CARNAUBA. Wax that is hard and durable and melts at 185°; it is excellent for giving wood a natural waxed finish.

CHAMFER. A bevel cut on the edge of a piece of wood.

CONTACT CEMENT. Any of the strong, rubbery adhesives which, when brushed on two surfaces and left to dry will grip on contact without clamping.

COUNTERSINK. Enlarging the top edge of a hole so head of screw or bolt can be brought flush with or recessed below the surface. Nails are "set" below the surface.

CROSSCUTTING. Cutting a piece of wood across the grain.

DADO. A wide groove or slot made on a power saw with a dado blade.

DANISH OIL. A popular oil finish for wood that is rubbed on to give a natural finish.

ESCUTCHEON PIN. A small decorative nail, usually brass and with a round head, used for attaching ornamental plates, small hinges, or metal corner caps.

EXTERIOR GRADE. Any plywood that is made with waterproof glue for use outdoors. It is usually stamped "Exterior" and/or has red marks on the ends of the sheet. (Interior plywood is stamped or marked green.) Marine plywood is top-grade exterior plywood with very minor or no imperfections.

FLAT GRAIN. Lumber in which the annual rings are at an angle of less than 45° to the surface. Common plywood is also flat grain, but is called rotary-cut because it is cut on huge lathes.

FLUTE. A decorative channel or groove cut in a column or a piece of furniture.

HALF-LAP. A joint formed by cutting away half the thicknesses of two pieces of wood so, when joined, their outer surfaces are flush.

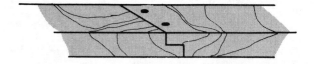

HARDBOARD. Any of the hard compressed sheets made of wood fiber, such as Masonite.

HOLLOW-CORE. A lightweight door that has a cellular construction sandwiched between two sheets of plywood.

JIG. A device that simplifies a hand or machine operation, usually by guiding tools or by use as a template.

KERF. The narrow cut made by a saw in wood. Kerfing is cutting a number of kerfs partway through a board crosswise so that you can bend it to a small radius.

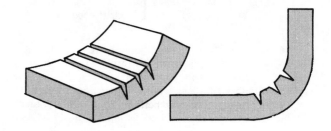

KILN-DRIED. Lumber that is artificially dried in a kiln to a "stable" moisture content. This moisture content varies with different woods.

LAMINATED PLASTIC. Any of the hard surfaced plastic sheets, such as Formica.

LAUAN. Another name for Philippine mahogany, used today to prevent confusion with Honduras mahogany, an entirely different wood.

LINEAL FEET. Pertaining to measuring and pricing lumber by its length. A 10-foot-long board or molding, whatever its width and thickness, is 10 lineal feet.

LUMBER-CORE. Plywood that has a thick core of solid wood, rather than several thin plys. Mainly used in furniture and cabinet work.

MITER. The joint formed by two beveled pieces of stock meeting at an angle.

MORTISE. A cavity or hole cut in a piece of wood to receive a tenon or tongue projecting from another piece —i.e., the mortise-and-tenon joint often used on furniture. Also the cavity cut in a cabinet or door for a lock.

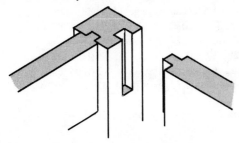

OPEN-GRAINED. Woods such as oak, walnut, and mahogany with pores that need to be filled to obtain a smooth finish. Close-grained woods are pine, fir, cedar, maple, etc.

PARTICLE-BOARD. Hard compressed sheets made of fair-sized chips of wood. It is usually thicker than hardboard and less subject to warpage than plywood.

PECKY. Any lumber which shows signs of decay. In our West today, the word usually refers to pecky cedar— lumber that has many holes but is firm and has been carefully finished and seasoned. Valued for wall paneling and some furniture.

PIN HINGE. A semi-invisible hinge very popular today for cabinets and furniture because it is easily installed.

PIN KNOT. A small knot or blemish that is ½ inch or less in diameter.

PRODUCTION PAPER. High-grade sandpaper, usually aluminum oxide, that cuts better and lasts longer than flint or garnet sandpaper.

RABBET. A groove cut along the edge or end of a board to receive another board.

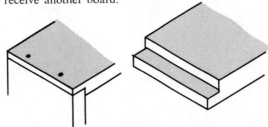

RAILS. In cabinet work, the horizontal pieces that support a table top or counter.

RESIN GLUE. Any modern glue that comes in powder form and is mixed with water. It is very strong; most types are fully waterproof.

RESORCINOL GLUES. The fully waterproof glues. Some come in two cans, to be mixed before they're used.

RIPPING. Cutting a board lengthwise.

ROUGH SAWN. Lumber that has been cut but not planed and exactly sized. The term also refers to lumber that has been carefully sized and seasoned, and to plywood that has one surface left rough sawn for the textured effect.

SCORE. To mark with notches, cuts, or lines.

SHEET: A full-size panel, usually 4 by 8 feet, of plywood or similar stock.

SOFTBOARD. The soft cellulose tiles and wall paneling.

SPLINE. A thin, flat strip of wood that is glued into pre-cut grooves to join two boards together.

SURFACED. Lumber which has been smoothed by a mill planer. S4S is a common abbreviation meaning surfaced on all four sides; S2S has been surfaced on two sides.

T & G. Any tongue-and-groove board, such as most flooring.

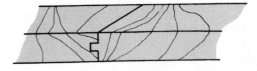

TOENAIL. To fasten surfaces with nails driven diagonally, usually from the side of one board into the flat of another.

VENEER. Any thin, one-ply sheet of wood. Also refers to paper-thin exotic woods with self-adhesive backings.

VERTICAL GRAIN. Lumber and plywood in which the annual rings are at an angle of 45° or more to the surface of the piece, rather than flat with it. Very popular in Douglas fir. Also called edge grain.

WARP AND WIND. A warped board is one that is concave in cross section—like a shallow trough. A board in wind has a twist in its length (also may be warped).

WHITE GLUE. Any of the various brands of white polyvinyl acetate glues. They come ready to use and have good holding power, but should not be exposed continually to sun or water.

PHOTOGRAPHERS

Bill Arbogast: page 74. **Craig Aurness:** page 22. **Ernest Braun:** page 27. **Steve Browning:** page 38. **Diana Bunce:** page 46. **Glenn M. Christiansen:** pages 5, 7 (top), 10, 11, 26, 42, 51, 56, 57 (bottom left), 59 (top), 64 (top, bottom left), 65, 70 (top), 72, 73, 76, 77 (top, center), 80 (bottom), 85, 89. **Richard Fish:** page 14 (top). **Gerald R. Fredrick:** page 86 (bottom). **Sherry Gellner:** page 18. **Walter Houk:** page 14 (bottom). **Russel Illig:** page 63. **Richard E. Londgren:** pages 24, 25, 48, 49. **John F. Marriott:** page 64 (bottom right). **Ells Marugg:** pages 6, 13, 87 (top), 90 (bottom). **Michael McGinnis:** page 15 (right). **Don Normark:** pages 69, 78, 79. **Norman A. Plate:** pages 4, 7 (bottom), 9, 31 (bottom), 44, 47, 68, 82 (bottom). **Tom Riley:** pages 16, 23 (bottom), 40, 41, 77 (bottom), 80 (top), 81. **Darrow M. Watt:** pages 12, 15 (left), 21, 23 (top), 28, 29, 30, 31 (top), 32, 33 (bottom), 34, 35, 36, 39, 50, 52, 53, 54, 55, 59 (bottom), 60, 62, 66, 67, 70 (bottom), 82 (top), 83, 84, 86 (top), 87 (bottom), 88, 90 (top), 91. **Peter O. Whiteley:** pages 8 (top), 33 (top), 57 (top, bottom right). **Craig Zwicky:** page 8 (bottom).

Front cover photograph by **Darrow M. Watt.** Back cover photographs by **Norman A. Plate** (top) and **Darrow M. Watt** (bottom).